named by God

overcoming your past,
transforming your present,
embracing your future

kasey van norman

TYNDALE HOUSE PUBLISHERS, INC.
CAROL STREAM, ILLINOIS

Visit Tyndale online at www.tyndale.com.

Visit Kasey Van Norman online at www.kaseyvannorman.com.

TYNDALE and Tyndale's quill logo are registered trademarks of Tyndale House Publishers, Inc.

Named by God Bible Study: Overcoming Your Past, Transforming Your Present, Embracing Your Future

Copyright © 2012 by Kasey Van Norman. All rights reserved.

Cover and author photographs taken by Stephen Vosloo. Copyright © Tyndale House Publishers, Inc. All rights reserved.

Designed by Daniel Farrell

Edited by Stephanie Rische

Published in association with literary agent Jenni Burke of D. C. Jacobson and Associates, an author management company, www.DCJacobson.com.

Unless otherwise indicated, all Scripture quotations are taken from the *Holy Bible*, New Living Translation, copyright © 1996, 2004, 2007 by Tyndale House Foundation. Used by permission of Tyndale House Publishers, Inc., Carol Stream, Illinois 60188. All rights reserved.

Scripture quotations marked NIV are taken from the Holy Bible, *New International Version,*® NIV.® Copyright © 1973, 1978, 1984, 2011 by Biblica, Inc.™ Used by permission of Zondervan. All rights reserved worldwide. www.zondervan.com.

Scripture quotations marked ESV are taken from *The Holy Bible*, English Standard Version® (ESV®), copyright © 2001 by Crossway, a publishing ministry of Good News Publishers. Used by permission. All rights reserved.

ISBN 978-1-4143-6475-9

Printed in the United States of America

18 17 16 15 14 13 12
7   6   5   4   3   2   1

Contents

Part III: Embracing Your Future

Before You Get Started

Some time ago I found myself sitting in a dark, confined place—in part because of the hurt others had caused me and in part because of my own sin. While there, I constantly breathed in the fumes of mildew and dirt. I was cramped, bruised, bloodied, thirsty, and covered in filth. My eyes became so adjusted to this place of darkness that I began to get comfortable there and settle in.

But, all glory to God, that hollow trench could never be my home. Why? Because long before the foundations of the earth were laid, my body was woven together with the greatest of divine detail (see Psalm 139). Long before the stars were mounted in the sky, I was given a *name*. The hands of the Creator shaped me and formed me, like a potter shapes his clay (see Isaiah 64:8). These hands embraced my unformed body with a love the human mind cannot possibly comprehend. These hands were palm pierced with the jagged edge of a condemning nail. And as the nail broke the flesh to penetrate muscle and bone, blood began to flow. The Savior's blood has spilled precious grace and mercy into my life—and that grace and mercy are available to everyone else who might reach for him.

Even in my darkest, dreariest times, those same hands were always there with me. Even in my loneliest moments, their presence was there to guide me. And when I finally chose to look up from my filth-covered habitat, those hands were reaching down for me, ushering me toward freedom. I had no strength to climb out on my own. I had been trying for so long, grasping and clawing at the dirt walls with all my might. But it wasn't until I placed my fingertips into the strong palms of my Savior that I was pulled into the light.

At first the light hurt my eyes, for it had been a while since I had beheld its brightness and beauty. But once my eyes adjusted, I ran toward the light and never looked back. He purified me from my sins that day; he washed me whiter than snow. He gave me back my joy and created in me a clean heart and a loyal spirit. He did not cast me from his presence but restored to me the joy of his salvation. He granted me a willingness to obey him (see Psalm 51:7-12).

From that moment forward, I committed to spending the rest of my earthly existence on a mission to teach his ways to others so they might turn back to him. I have vowed that, until I reach eternity, I will live a life radically for him, singing his songs of righteousness and declaring his praise. My spirit and heart were broken before him, and in that brokenness he was pleased (see Psalm 51:13-19).

For many years I questioned why certain experiences had to take place in my life, why I have had this burning passion in my heart to boldly profess his name despite my deep failings. But I have come to believe that God has good plans for his children—plans to redeem even the most hopeless of situations. I know now that I could not effectively write of the Lord's healing and restoration post-sin had I not personally experienced it. And I could not effectively challenge other believers to live radically reformed lives for Christ had I not made the same commitment myself.

This study began as a weekly devotional for the ladies in my small group at church and as a tool of healing in my own life. And now, loved one, as you embark on this journey with me, my prayer remains the same—that, by the time you reach the end of this study, you will be transformed from the person you were at the beginning of week 1. I pray that God's Word—his very breath of life—will become so intoxicating to you that it will be like an addictive drug. I pray these daily readings from the Bible will develop a consistent pattern in your life and you will begin to crave the Scriptures like never before.

I also pray that you will allow the power of the resurrected Christ to overcome every area of your life that is ruled by the flesh, that you will give him the authority to transform your present state. Whether you are fresh out of the darkness of sin or your toes are dangling on the edge of a drop-off or you're just feeling a little complacent in your relationship with God, my hope is that, as you study the Word of God, you will experience a more intimate relationship with your Savior.

Before you proceed, allow me to offer one word of caution: you must want this! If you aren't desperate for a deeper connection with Christ, save yourself the time and money, and put this book back on the shelf. Our Redeemer desires a relationship with us that is far beyond our earthly imaginations. But in return, he requires our complete abandon—our letting go of self and all that this world has to offer. Are you willing to make this kind of all-out commitment?

If you're ready to work, your world is about to be rocked! If you've ever felt in bondage to your past, you are about to break those chains. If you've ever felt unprepared to serve God and others, you are about to be equipped. If you have ever questioned your purpose or meaning in life, you are about to discover God's plans for your future.

As we dive into this adventure together, I promise that I won't ask you to go anywhere I haven't already gone myself. Come on, what are you waiting for? I can tell you from personal experience that the water's exhilarating!

How to Use This Study

The God of the universe desires to speak to you, yes *you*, through the pages of his Word. And I believe he can use the next six weeks as you go through this study to bring permanent change into the depths of your soul.

This study is full of interactive exercises. And due to the fact that I am a no-fluff, to-the-point kind of girl, these exercises are meant to be challenging. They have been handcrafted with the intent of helping you peel back your layers and deal with them from a supernatural perspective. Didn't think you had any layers to peel back? Well, friend, from my own collisions with the human condition, I have learned that we've got more barricades around our hearts than an army platoon under attack. And on top of that, we don't readily allow other people past our barricades—not those who love us, and not even the one who knows us better than we know ourselves. So as we take the first steps on this journey, it is vital that we tackle each exercise fearlessly.

This study is a six-week interactive experience between you and the Creator. Ideally, though, you'll get the most out of it within the huddle of a group—whether through your church, a small group, or just a gang of your closest buddies who want to get together each week. Each week in this book contains a group session for you to discuss with other people as well as five individual encounters for you to work through with God. (Since I was never a big fan of homework in school, I try not to use words like *assignments*.)

Each group session will take anywhere from thirty to forty minutes, including the video session. I have kept the questions in these sessions to a minimum since my desire is for you to connect with the other individuals in your group. In addition to completing the questions, I encourage you to allow adequate time for prayer and group discussion.

I have clocked the daily encounters, which are designed for you to do alone, to take somewhere between twenty-five and forty minutes each, depending on how deep you choose to go.

Here are the materials and resources you'll need to get the most of this study.

1. *Named by God Video Curriculum* (one per group)

Through a live teaching DVD, I will personally walk with you through each group session as I challenge you, get vulnerable with you, and do everything I can to love on you from a distance. Each week's video portion is approximately thirty to forty minutes in length. After watching the live teaching session, dig deep and get real with one another as you discuss the group-session questions.

With the exception of the first group session, be sure to come fully prepared to each group experience. When you make it a priority to complete each daily encounter as thoughtfully as your heart and hand can muster, the experience will be much richer for you and for the rest of the group.

If your circumstances don't allow you to participate in this study with a group, it is still possible to complete it alone. Because God designed us to work and grow in relation to other humans, the group route is obviously the most rewarding, but God can use his Word to speak to his children under any kind of circumstances.

2. *Named by God Leader's Guide* (one per group)

If you are the head of the group, I highly recommend that you get a copy of the leader's guide to help you facilitate discussions and to give you tips about shepherding God's people. As someone who has held the role of small-group leader for a number of years, I have utmost respect for anyone serving in this way.

At the beginning of each week's study, I speak to you from my heart through a note of encouragement and give you an idea of what to expect in the week ahead. I provide you with specific Scriptures that will speak to you as the leader, as well as a recommended timeline, a schedule, and discussion questions to use during your group session. And since I have been on both the leader and the participant side of studies, I also include insights on dealing with the various group responses and personalities you may encounter over the six-week study.

Ultimately, my prayer is that this tool helps you find clarity and confidence as you go forward on this journey with the Lord, equipped and armed for the joyful challenge of being a group leader.

3. Your own Bible

For both the group sessions and the individual encounters, you will need a Bible you are comfortable reading. Don't stress about the translation—it doesn't have to be the same as mine or the other participants' in your group. Just bring a Bible you feel drawn to and one you can understand easily. I will primarily be using the New Living Translation (NLT) in the video sessions and in the study. As a side note, some of my faves are the NLT, the English Standard Version (ESV), the New International Version (NIV), and the New American Standard Bible (NASB).

If you don't have a Bible, get one! If cost is a factor, talk to people at your church and see if they can help you out.

4. Other resources

I'd also recommend that you have a pen and a journal handy for both the group and the individual portions. Of course, you are welcome to write in this book, but if you're like me, you might write all over the lines and white space of a book and still need more. Oh, and you might need tissues at some point too (my previous participants asked me to include this one for you).

5. *Named by God* book

If you're interested in taking this experience to a whole new, supernatural level, I encourage you to add one additional tool—*Named by God*, the book. This book was written to be read alongside the Bible study. Within the book I go deeper into my own story—my own painful experiences, pitfalls, rebellion, and doubts—as well as my breaking point of surrender that ultimately led to God's grace-filled redemption, healing, and restoration in my life. I also dig further into Scripture to follow people from the Bible and to see how God used the brokenness of their lives to bring out his redemptive purposes. Along the way, we'll learn how to let these truths sink into our lives too.

As you read my book, you may be surprised to find pieces of my journey reflecting your own life in some way. I have a hunch this is the place where you and I may bond like two friends crying our eyes out together at a small corner table over coffee. Perhaps my story will shake you up a bit— it may catch you off guard, cause you to do some spiritual double takes, and even resonate inside you in a place you haven't dared to look in years. In any case, I have no doubt we will laugh together, cry together, get our toes stepped on together, and most important, be moved to a new place of intimacy with our God together.

The book is intended to unite my story, your story, and God's Word as we draw closer to who we are meant to be—to find our true identity and purpose in him. To help guide you on this journey, I have included in this Bible study the specific chapters from the *Named by God* book to read in conjunction with each week of the study.

• • •

Before we proceed, here is my official checklist you must go through to see if you are tall enough to ride this ride. If you can say, "Check!" to at least one of the following, I hereby clear you for takeoff:

☐ I have never done a Bible study before, but I would like to grow in my walk with Jesus.

☐ I have participated in many Bible studies before, but I realize there is still so much for me to learn about the Lord.

☐ I have trouble reading my Bible on my own and am worried I won't understand what I am reading.

☐ I have been reading my Bible faithfully for many years, and I am looking forward to a fresh take on Scripture.

☐ I am not sure where I stand with Jesus. I think I am a Christian and am going to heaven, but how can I know for sure?

☐ I know beyond a shadow of a doubt that I will spend eternity with Jesus, but I would love to know how to better serve him and live out his purpose for me until that time.

☐ I have such a horrible past that I am unsure there is any hope left for me. I am timid and scared to share my story with my group for fear of being judged.

☐ I have worked through much of my past with the Lord already, but I would love to know how to better connect with others who are hurting and confused.

☐ I don't know exactly why I'm here—my friend dragged me along.

The truth is, whether you are a seminary grad or a street grad or anyone in between, this Bible study is for you! So what are we waiting for? Let's get started.

Part I:
Overcoming Your Past

Week 1

Introduction

Recommended Reading From *Named by God*: Introduction, chapters 1–3
Named by God Video Curriculum: DVD Session 1

As followers of Christ, some of us have no idea just how much power we have through Jesus. Here's what we need to understand: who we *are* doesn't determine how we act; who we *think* we are determines how we act. And for so many of us, our thought processes remain tainted by past disappointments, suffering, and hardship.

If we think we are mistakes, we will go through life making mistakes. If we think we are undeserving, we will live defeated lives. If we think we must spend all our time running from our pasts, we will live in a continual state of chaos. And if we think we are only by-products of other people's sin, we will keep choosing sin over the power God offers.

Let me fill you in on a truth about your past: God wants to use it to set the stage for a miracle in your present. Believe me—anyone God has ever raised up in the present had a history of some kind of sin and disappointment in his or her past.

When God comes to Moses in Exodus 3 and a bush begins to burn with the glory of God, Moses (whose past includes murder) responds with, "Who am I to appear before Pharaoh? Who am I to lead the people of Israel out of Egypt?" (verse 11). When God appears to Isaiah in chapter 6 of the book Isaiah, the prophet's response to God is, "It's all over! I am doomed, for I am a sinful man. I have filthy lips, and I live among a people with filthy lips" (verse 5). In Luke 5:8, when Jesus does a large-scale miracle for his disciples (former fishermen with no real training or prestige), Peter exclaims, "Oh, Lord, please leave me—I'm too much of a sinner to be around you."

These responses are on track—we *should* be increasingly aware of our sin the closer we get to God's holiness. Yes, we are sinful. Yes, we have a past that is filled with sins we've committed against others and sins others have committed against us. Yes, we've disappointed others, and others have disappointed us. We have all fractured the image of God. But . . . (That's one of my favorite words in the Bible—*but.*)

This week we will begin to lay the groundwork for the "but" in your life.

You are unworthy, *but* . . .
You come from a broken home, *but* . . .

You are a sinner, *but* . . .
You have a past, *but* . . .
You have become completely stagnant in your relationship with the Lord, *but* . . .

● ● ●

This week is all about going back before we can move forward—recognizing where we come from so we can think clearly about where we are going. Once we can get our heads on straight about who we are in Christ, we can then begin to live in Christ's power on a daily basis.

We begin our journey with an overview of who we were at birth, as well as who has influenced us since then. I told you this wasn't going to be light and fluffy! This week is perhaps one of the most difficult of our journey together, so let's go in fighting. Commit to following through and being persistent. Be prayerful, accurate, and thorough as you read each passage and complete each exercise. Keep in mind that you only have one audience—this book is between you and God alone. He is the only one who will be checking your answers, and he expects complete openness and honesty. See it through to the end, my friend—and don't forget we're in this together.

Group Session 1

(To be completed along with the *Named by God* video curriculum, preferably in a group setting.)

To fully grasp what it means to live as one named by God, it is critical that we start our journey at the beginning—yes, I mean the *literal* beginning. You may think Genesis is simply the story of a fellow named Adam and a gal named Eve, but the truth is, you and I are just as much the main characters as they are.

Our role in this story begins in Genesis 3. If you fail to understand this chapter, nothing in the Bible—or in your life—will make sense.

1. **You must understand your adversary for three reasons:**

   He is _____ than you.

   He has more _____ than you.

   He is bent on _____ you.

2. **First Satan's strategy is to target your freewill hub—your** _____ .

   The LORD God placed the man in the Garden of Eden to tend and watch over it. But the LORD God warned him, "You may freely eat the fruit of every tree in the garden—except the tree of the knowledge of good and evil. If you eat its fruit, you are sure to die."   GENESIS 2:15-17

   Satan wants you to overlook all of your freedom and focus in on the one restriction.

3. **Next, Satan wants to plant a seed of** _____ **in your mind of God's faithfulness.**

4. **Third, Satan will direct you to the one lie that has plagued human history since Genesis 3—that you can be your own** _____ **and not face any consequences—otherwise known as** _____ .

5

5. Satan wants to create an atmosphere for you to linger in _____ just long enough for you to sin.

So what's your fig leaf?

Our sin is the problem. But we can't see that because of our pride.

The man—Adam—named his wife Eve, because she would be the mother of all who live. And the LORD God made clothing from animal skins for Adam and his wife. Then the LORD God said, "Look, the human beings have become like us, knowing both good and evil. What if they reach out, take fruit from the tree of life, and eat it? Then they will live forever!" So the LORD God banished them from the Garden of Eden, and he sent Adam out to cultivate the ground from which he had been made. GENESIS 3:20-23

6. God made our very first parents, Adam and Eve, and we are a _____ of that.

You were dead because of your sins and because your sinful nature was not yet cut away. Then God made you alive with Christ, for he forgave all our sins. He canceled the record of the charges against us and took it away by nailing it to the cross. In this way, he disarmed the spiritual rulers and authorities. He shamed them publicly by his victory over them on the cross. COLOSSIANS 2:13-15

Day 1

....

Just Born with It

No matter who we are or how we grew up, all of humanity has this in common: we're all born as a result of the union of one man and one woman. Each of us has a mother and a father. Whether they are current heroes in your life or you've never seen their faces, the fact remains that you are a genetic product of your parents' union. For some of us, childhood and adolescence were shaped by the two people who match our DNA. Others grew up in an environment with just one person or no one who shares our bloodline.

I would love to spend time unpacking the various backgrounds we might have been raised in. But for the purpose of this study, we will focus on one word to describe the people who have known us "since we were knee high," as my grandfather would say: *family*. Like it or not, if we are going to talk out our pasts, we have to address that tricky topic.

At this point, some of you are breathing a sigh of relief. You're thinking, *Okay, I can handle this. I grew up in a good Christian home. My parents stayed together. I had everything I needed, and I was taught to know God and to walk in his ways.* And to that I say, "Praise God!" As a parent myself, I know how difficult it can be to pray for and direct your children in this dark world. I thank God for the parents who call on him for guidance as they take on the big responsibility of training the next generation. But even if you had a positive childhood experience, I believe you'll benefit from looking into your past.

For others, the very thought of discussing family may sound terrifying. You may be thinking, *What family? My dad left my mom for another woman when I was a kid. My mom had to work three jobs just to provide for us, which left her no time for making supper, let alone offering spiritual guidance. My siblings and I had to take care of ourselves . . . and we still do!*

Wherever you find yourself, I'd like to encourage you to take a moment to pray. Ask God to grant you a very real look at your family—the people who raised you. I want you to think about your childhood, your teenage years, or any season when you relied on someone else to provide for you and protect you. If there are mental roadblocks, simply ask God for a clear, objective picture of your family.

We're going to spend some time thinking about how our families have shaped the people we are. But before we begin, take the opportunity to pray through your upbringing, thanking God for the good parts and asking him to redeem the broken ones.

1. Think of three significant events from your past that have influenced who you are today. What would it look like for God to redeem those situations? It's just you and the Lord right now—allow him to reveal these truths to you.

_____

_____

_____

_____

_____

_____

2. Okay, you got it? Now fill in the following information to the best of your ability.

Your name (given at birth)

_____

Biological father's name (if known)

_____

Biological mother's name (if known)

_____

Father figure's name (if different from above)

_____

Mother figure's name (if different from above)

_____

List siblings or other family members (if any) who lived with you at any time in your household.

_____

_____

_____

Now, this next step may take a little effort, especially if your childhood came with its set of challenges. But hang in there and trust God to give you revelation and to be there with you.

I don't know about you, but in my home we collect a _lot_ of trash. Dirty diapers, uneaten food, credit card applications—you name it! Once my husband takes the trash to the curb, though, I forget about it—out of sight, out of mind. But guess what? The guys who get paid to pick it up and haul it away from my house don't forget about it. They have to remember, or else it will build up on my front lawn in a smelly, nasty pile of filth.

So this is my challenge to you today. We don't need to wallow in or get buried by our trash, but we can't just ignore it. We have to sort through it to find what we need to get rid of and what we need to keep. We can't just put it outside and forget about it—we have to allow God to deal with it for good.

Come on—let's dig together.

Now we are going to gather a bit more information about the people we listed. In the next section I have designated a place for mother, father, and siblings. Under each heading, I want you to think of at least three traits—positive and negative—that this person possessed. Whether that characteristic made a direct impact on your life or not, write down what you are able to remember. These traits can be personality attributes, behaviors, or lifestyle patterns. Do your best to keep your emotions out of it; try to be as factual as possible. If any recollection is a bit fuzzy, don't write it down. To get you started, I have shared a few of my own family memories.

Mother (or Mother Figure)

Positive traits:
Put my siblings and me first; supported us in everything we did; loved the Lord

Negative traits:
Divorced my father; struggled with her sense of self-worth; carried a lot of guilt

Father (or Father Figure)

Positive traits:
Hard worker; dependable; enjoyed keeping things clean and functioning well

Negative traits:
Workaholic; struggled to display his love; struggled with losing his temper

Now it's your turn.

Mother (or Mother Figure)

Positive traits:

_____

_____

_____

_____

_____

Negative traits:

_____

_____

_____

_____

_____

Father (or Father Figure)

Positive traits:

_____

_____

_____

_____

_____

Negative traits:

_____

_____

_____

_____

_____

Siblings (or Others Present in Your Home)

Name:

Positive traits:

_____

_____

_____

_____

_____

Negative traits:

_____

_____

_____

_____

_____

Name:

Positive traits:

_____

_____

_____

_____

_____

Negative traits:

_____

_____

_____

_____

_____

Name:

Positive traits:

_____

_____

_____

_____

_____

Negative traits:

_____

_____

_____

_____

_____

3. Look back at your lists. How have traits and behaviors of your family members (both positive and negative) impacted the choices you've made and continue to make in your life?

_____

_____

_____

_____

_____

4. In what ways do you blame your family members for the person you've become?

_____

_____

_____

_____

_____

_____

_____

5. In what ways do you credit your family members for the person you've become?

_____

_____

_____

_____

_____

_____

6. Read Psalm 51:5. From what point were you considered sinful?

_____

7. Now read Ephesians 2:1-3. This is Paul's picture of one who has yet to come to faith in Christ—a lost sinner! You see, people who are outside a relationship with Jesus are dead spiritually; they are unable to recognize and respond to spiritual things. Not only are these people dead on the inside, but they are also enslaved by Satan and the enticements of this world. Everyone is born with a bent toward evil.

Complete this portion of verse 3: "All of us used to live that way, following the passionate desires and inclinations of our sinful _____ ," or "gratifying the cravings of our _____ " (NIV).

As we look to our family members and the traits that have impacted who we are today, we must understand our personal nature upon arriving into the human family. No matter who we were born to or how they raised us, the very nature we were born with is corrupted.

I know this may sound harsh, but it's true.

8. Read Romans 5:14.

This verse states that Adam is a _____ of the one to come.

9. Now read Romans 5:15-19.

Meditate for a moment on verse 18, and let's end our day together in prayer. Perhaps you might pray something like this:

Father, I know that because of Adam and Eve's sin, all humanity is condemned and bent toward evil from birth. I know that I, too, would have disobeyed you just as they did had I been in the Garden that day with the serpent. I praise you, Lord, that although Adam's sin plunged the human race into death, we are freely offered salvation and life through your Son, Jesus! Thank you that, although my past is marked by the sins of my family as I grew up—and by my own sin—in your grace and mercy you have seen fit to rescue me. Thank you for moving me forward into a life of victory over the grave and freedom from all sinful cravings and addictions. Thank you for my parents and family members, despite their shortcomings and failures. Help me to see you clearly through the love of those who surrounded me. I give you the glory for the lessons you've taught me through them along the way. In Jesus' name, amen.

Day 2

....

Susceptible to Infection

As we begin today, ask God to give you a soft heart toward your family members. Pray that God will give you the grace-filled eyes of Christ so you can see them as he sees them.

Read Exodus 20:5-6; then read Exodus 34:4-7. Before we go any further, let's take a moment to grasp the awesomeness of the scene painted for us in chapter 34.

1. **How did the Lord choose to communicate with Moses?**

_____ The Lord stood a long way off and yelled.

_____The Lord spoke to Moses in his spirit as Moses meditated.

_____The Lord stood there with Moses and proclaimed his own name.

Can you even begin to imagine the Lord of the universe standing next to you in order to give you a message? And as he passes in front of you, his voice resounds in your ears? It gives me holy goose bumps to imagine what the voice of the Lord would sound like!

2. **List the personal characteristics the Lord expresses in Exodus 34:6-7.**

_____

_____

_____

The Lord has the ability, if he desires, to rain down fire from the sky, split the ground on which Moses is standing, or cause every aspect of his creation to bow down in worship of his majesty and glory. Instead, God chooses this personal, intimate way to give Moses a glimpse of his character.

3. **Fill in the blanks to the second part of verse 7.**

I do not excuse the guilty. I lay the sins of the _____ upon their

_____ and grandchildren; the entire family is affected—even children

in the third and fourth generations.

4. **Go back and reread Exodus 20:5-6. Fill in the blanks below.**

I, the LORD your God, am a jealous God. . . . I lay the sins of the _____ upon

their _____ ; the entire family is affected—even children in the third and

fourth generations of those who reject me. But I lavish unfailing _____ for

a thousand generations on those who love me and obey my commands.

5. **Read Ezekiel 18:17-20. What will happen to the child who has done what is "just and right"?**

_____

_____

6. **In fact, the child will not share in his or her parents'** _____ .

7. **Which of the following metaphors sounds like you? Place a check next to the one that best describes you.**

_____ Drunk: I recognize that I am deeply involved in a pattern of sin that very much resembles that of a close family member. I don't know how to stop—or maybe I'm not willing to.

_____ Recovering Alcoholic: Although I followed for a time in the sinful footsteps of certain family members, I have since repented. I am still tempted at times to engage in this behavior, but I'm trying to obey the Lord instead.

_____ Designated Driver: Regardless of a family member's continued pattern of sin in my home, I have stayed focused on the Lord, never following in that behavior.

8. **What generational curses have been passed on to you?**

_____

_____

_____

_____

_____

_____

9. **In what ways has your infection impacted your life and the lives of others?**

_____

_____

_____

_____

_____

_____

_____

_____

_____

10. What generational curses do you want to be sure stop with you?

_____

_____

_____

_____

_____

_____

_____

_____

11. Circle any of the following that pertain to your family, whether in the past or in the present. Be honest, and remember that the only one who matters already knows the answers.

adultery	homosexuality
alcoholism	hypocrisy
anger	jealousy
anxiety	materialism
bitterness	pornography
blame	premarital sex
criticism	pride
depression	selfishness
discontentment	self-pity
dishonesty	sexual abuse
divorce	substance abuse
emotional abuse	workaholism
gossip	worry
greed	

Day 3

Royal Mischief

Begin this time in prayer, asking God to give you insight about the traits that have been passed on to you from the home you were raised in. As you spend some time meditating on your childhood, think about this question: What sins have a stronghold in your life because you witnessed them throughout the years as you grew and matured? Ask God to reveal not only the obvious sins but also the ones that are more difficult to detect, such as worry, self-pity, and pride. When God brings these sins to the forefront of your mind, don't lose heart. If you have repented of the sin, it is gone—as far as the east is from the west. But even though we can receive complete forgiveness, God doesn't want us to forget our sin completely. He has granted his children memories so we won't continue to skin our knees over and over again.

Read 2 Samuel 13 (that's right—the whole chapter!).

Whew! I don't know about you, but I feel better. Why, you might ask? Before we break down this passage, let's get real for a moment. You have to admit that it feels pretty good to read about people in the Bible—families that were part of the royal line, God's chosen ones—who were just as messed up as we are today!

In the first eleven chapters of 2 Samuel we discover how God empowered David to defeat Israel's enemies and expand his kingdom. But we also discover a darker side in chapter 11—David's sin of adultery with Bathsheba and the subsequent killing of her husband, Uriah. We now come to a place in the royal story where David wrestles with the aftermath of his sin. It comes in a way we might not expect—in the form of sibling rivalry.

1. What are the names of the two *A* sons of David recorded in 2 Samuel 13:1?

_____ and _____

Although Absalom and Amnon play the lead roles in this story, there are actually three heirs to David's throne: Amnon (David's firstborn), Absalom (David's third son), and Adonijah (David's fourth son). Tamar is King David's daughter. The book of 2 Samuel gives a breathtaking account of how a holy God responds to the vulnerability of the human condition through the person of David.

The same is as true for us today as it was for David: the Lord is always faithful to forgive, but the consequences of sin can be excruciating.

But back to our story. We find out in chapter 13 that Amnon develops a perverted love for his half sister Tamar. At this time Tamar is a virgin princess kept in seclusion from all other men, including her male relatives, until she can be given in marriage.[1] Therefore, we know Amnon must build up quite an imagination as he daydreams about his half sister.

2. **According to 2 Samuel 13:1-4, how does Amnon describe his feelings for Tamar?**

_____

_____

_____

_____

3. **Who becomes the mastermind behind the malicious plan to get Tamar alone with her brother Amnon? Check out verses 3-7.**

_____

_____

_____

_____

4. **Let me ask you a personal question here: When you're going through a tough time and you need some advice, who do you turn to? List the top three sources from whom you seek guidance in the rough patches of your life. (You may give initials here if you prefer.)**

_____

_____

_____

_____

Gut Check Time

5. **Looking back at your list, was the name God or Jesus the first on your list? If not, why do you think he was overlooked?**

_____

_____

_____

_____

---

[1] According to Robert Jamieson, A. R. Fausset, and David Brown in *Commentary Critical and Explanatory on the Whole Bible* (Zondervan, 1984), "unmarried daughters were kept in close seclusion from the company of men; no strangers, nor even their relatives of the other sex, being permitted to see them without the presence of witnesses."

6. Do you have a family member anywhere in the top three? What do you see as the pros and cons for turning to a family member for counsel in your times of need or despair?

_____

_____

_____

_____

God can certainly use other people to counsel us and guide us when we need help. Proverbs 27:9 tells us that the heartfelt counsel of a friend is sweet. Personally, I don't know where I would be without the godly advice, prayer, and accountability from close friends, family members, and mentors throughout my life. But I also know the heartache I bring on myself when I go to other people first with my issues.

We must keep in mind that even our most beloved friends and trusted advisers are made from the same bits of dust we are. We need to seek the Lord's counsel first and foremost and then trust him to bring people to speak truth into our lives.

7. I love this insight from Job 12:12-13:

Wisdom belongs to the aged,
and understanding to the old.

But true wisdom and power are found in God;
counsel and understanding are his.

What strikes you about this Scripture passage? What does it say about human wisdom versus the wisdom of God?

_____

_____

_____

_____

_____

_____

_____

_____

Day 4

....

David's Unruly Bunch

Welcome back, friends. Let's begin today's study in prayer, casting Satan from our thoughts and our time here in God's Word. We will be filling the air with the sound of crinkled paper today as we devour the pages of the living Word of God. Pray that God gives you the desire to see this encounter through to the end. There is a blessing in store for you today!

We ended day 3 at a climactic point of the story in 2 Samuel 13.

Here's a brief recap: Brother Amnon has a serious case of lust, which he believes to be love, for his half sister Tamar. Amnon is so consumed with this "love" for Tamar that he is practically making himself sick—not eating, not sleeping, and walking around the palace looking just plain wretched. As pitiful as this sounds, be honest: have *you* been there? Fortunately, I can laugh at myself now when I look back at the ridiculous tears I shed and brown-bag lunches I refused to eat over some dramatic high school heartbreak! *Of course* I was in love with him after only two weeks and a spin around the parking lot in his 1987 Camaro!

Let's break here for a little pop quiz.

• Although Amnon is the one who is desperate, who thinks up the plan to "help" Amnon?

_____

• What adjective does the Bible use to describe Jonadab in verse 3?

_____

• What does Jonadab tell Amnon to do in verse 5?

_____

_____

_____

• As the plan is thrown into action, who shows up on the scene to check on his ailing son (verse 6)?

_____

• Amnon must have been putting on quite a show as he was laid up in bed, based on David's reaction in verse 7. How does David respond to Amnon's request?

_____ He tells Amnon there is no need to bother Tamar; he will simply have the royal chef bring Amnon's food.

_____ He decides to spend the extra time with his son in his illness and serve him the food himself.

_____ He has a servant tell Tamar to come to her brother's royal suite just to make him some bread.

Okay, the pop quiz is over. Good job!

Amnon certainly took being "lovesick" to a new level, trying to fake out everyone, including dear old Dad. I can't help but wonder if Amnon was thinking to himself, *Well, if my dad can get away with adultery and murder and still be king, then surely I, the king's son, can get away with rape.* As we pick apart the following verses, we begin to see the pollution that overflows from a parent's bad example.

1. In 2 Samuel 13:9 we read, "When she set the serving tray before him, he _____

_____ ."

Then Amnon orders everyone else out of the room, and that's when it happens. Tamar has done nothing wrong, yet in a single moment, she is raped, violated, and disgraced—and in her culture, that means she's destined for a future of pain and humiliation. (As a side note to all you singles wondering when your true love will come, please know that someone who truly loves you will never—and I mean *never*—justify violating your body, mind, emotions, or moral standards in order to satisfy his selfish appetite.)

That's not the end of Tamar's story. Wouldn't you know that, after Amnon takes advantage of her, he no longer wants her!

2. According to verse 15, Amnon's love has turned into what?

_____

_____

3. This graphic scene ends with the news getting back to Dad in verse 21. In this verse we read that David is _____ .

I keep expecting something after this reaction—some kind of discipline or words of wisdom from a father to his rebellious son. Some message to the effect of, "You are seriously stupid if you think I'm going to let you get away with this!"

4. Instead, we read in verse 23 that how much time passes after this horrible incident takes place?

_____

_____

It turns out that, after King David hears about his son's mischief, he has a natural, fatherly reaction to it. However, what happens next is possibly the most tragic of all parenting maneuvers—he does nothing.

We don't know this for sure from Scripture, but perhaps David's memory of his own sin plagues him with such guilt and shame that he feels unworthy to discipline his children for similar failings. Perhaps he thinks the scene too closely resembles his own rebellion, and he feels powerless to punish Amnon for it.

Either way, it is clear that King David is reaping the generational consequences of his sin. Some time before, God had given him this warning through the prophet Nathan: "Your family will live by the sword because you have despised me by taking Uriah's wife to be your own. This is what the LORD says: Because of what you have done, I will cause your own household to rebel against you" (2 Samuel 12:10-11).

5. **When you hear of another person (perhaps someone from your church, workplace, or community) committing a sin that is uncharacteristic of anything you believe you would ever do (murder, theft, adultery, etc.), what are the first thoughts and emotions that come to you?**

I tend to think . . .

_____

_____

_____

_____

I tend to feel . . .

_____

_____

_____

_____

6. **How does your reaction change if the sin is something that has been a stronghold in your life at some point—in other words, something you can personally relate to?**

I tend to think . . .

_____

_____

_____

_____

I tend to feel . . .

_____

_____

_____

_____

Time to Rewind

Let's go back in time a bit and see how David ended up in this position of power in the first place.

7. **Read 1 Samuel 16:10-13.**

Although Samuel anoints David with oil, who anoints him with power?

_____

_____

8. **Now read 2 Samuel 7:8-16. Fill in the following blanks below.**

The Lord tells David he will make his name _____ (verse 9).

God will provide a _____ for the people of Israel so they will no longer be disturbed (verse 10).

The Lord will grant David _____ from all his enemies (verse 11).

The Lord will _____ one of David's descendants, or offspring (verse 12).

Throughout the past two days we have seen only a small glimpse into the person of David, but it has been enough to see that he has some glaring sins and has tumbled headfirst into some serious pits. Yet the Lord doesn't revoke his calling as a "man after [God's] own heart" (1 Samuel 13:14). Despite David's sin and the sin of his children, God is willing to use David to accomplish his perfect purpose of salvation through the coming Messiah.

As I think upon my own sinful rebellion and disobedience, as well as the sin I was subjected to from previous generations, I am encouraged by David's story. If the Lord can use a dysfunctional family like David's, complete with their faults and failures, surely he can use my family and me, too.

Before we leave our time together, I'd like to encourage you to offer a closing prayer to the Lord. Perhaps it might sound something like this:

> *Father, it is so easy for me to blame others for the pain and hurt I am experiencing today. I admit that I have been carrying around feelings of bitterness, anger, and resentment toward one or more of my family members. Lord, remind me that you intend the consequences of sin to be used as discipline—to chasten those you love so they return to your embrace. Make me ever mindful of my own sinful tendencies so that, through your grace, they may not trickle down to the next generation— whether my children or someone else's. Humble me as I draw closer to you. Give me the strength to take my eyes off those around me and those who came before me and instead place my focus firmly on you. May I take responsibility for myself, knowing that I will stand before you and you alone. In Jesus' name, amen.*

Day 5

When Love and Truth Collide

Begin today with a prayer, asking God to reveal his love to you—a love you might be taking for granted. You will never be able to love other people well if you haven't experienced God's love yourself. Also ask God to clearly show you the areas of your life that need a makeover, starting with the foundation of love.

When a Pharisee asks Jesus what the most important commandment is, his reply revolves around love. He says, "'You must love the LORD your God with all your heart, all your soul, and all your mind.' This is the first and greatest commandment. A second is equally important: 'Love your neighbor as yourself.' The entire law and all the demands of the prophets are based on these two commandments" (Matthew 22:37-40).

1. **Place a *yes* or *no* in the blank next to each statement as it applies to you today. Be completely honest with yourself.**

_____ I have feelings of guilt, shame, or regret that consume me for the better part of the day.

_____ I feel unequipped to give godly counsel to anyone struggling with sin because of the guilt I carry for my own sin.

_____ I feel unworthy to attend church, serve in ministry, or get close to other Christians because of my past mistakes.

_____ I would prefer not to communicate with a particular family member due to the resentment I harbor toward him or her.

_____ On at least a weekly basis, I dwell on the wrongs done to me by a family member.

_____ I regularly withhold love from a particular person in my life because of the hurt he or she has caused me.

_____ I desire revenge on a person who has deeply wounded me.

_____ I struggle with a habitual pattern of sin in my life.

_____ I blame a family member or someone from my past for the current sin in my life.

_____ I feel powerless and scared to confront my sinful patterns.

_____ I feel spiritually numb.

_____ I have no desire to confront the sin in my life.

Sweet child of God, I pray that, as you reflect on this list, you'll accept love from one infected person to another. And let me give you this warning: if you answered yes to just one of those items, you are in need of your scheduled dose of antibiotics! In other words, you're not allowing the love God offers you to fully reign in your life. Like many medications, this love has side effects. When it starts seeping into your veins, it affects your speech, your behavior, and the way you respond to circumstances and other people.

2. **Read Ephesians 3:19.**

The love of Christ . . . is too great to _____ fully.

3. **Read Ephesians 4:26-32.**

If you are having trouble accepting God's love or expressing love to others, it may be because you are holding on to feelings of anger and resentment over past wrongs.

When you play the blame game and become consumed with anger, who gets a foothold (verse 27)? _____

Who is grieved when you allow the past to dictate your present (verse 30)?

_____

You are to forgive and move on, just as _____ through _____ has forgiven you (verse 32).

4. **Read Romans 8:9-11 and reread Matthew 22:37-39.**

If you know that you are a new creation in Christ, then according to Romans 8:9, who is now living in you?

_____

_____

What does Jesus say is the first and greatest commandment (see Matthew 22:37)?

_____

_____

What is the second greatest commandment (verse 39)?

_____

_____

If you are coming to this point in our journey together and there is a person from your past (a parent, a sibling, a grandparent, etc.) you haven't been able to forgive, I encourage you to take a few moments right now to look at this relationship through the eyes of truth and love.

Truth: You will never be fully whole and healthy while carrying around baggage from the past.

Love: True forgiveness that sets you free can only come through the channel of love.

Truth: Love and forgiveness have nothing to do with a feeling. It's perfectly natural to not feel like loving and forgiving someone, but that isn't a valid excuse for not doing it.

Love: We can let go when people hurt us, not because of a feeling or because they deserve it, but because God gives us the power to do so.

Truth: When it comes down to it, you are no better than the person who hurt you.

Love: When Jesus came to this earth, he was unjustly accused, beaten until his flesh was raw, spat upon, mocked, and unjustly murdered. And yet, out of his incomprehensible love for us, he reached down to lavish his grace, mercy, and redemption on us.

Bondage breaking can only take place if we are willing to make the courageous and breathtaking choice to lay it down. *What is* it? you may wonder. Well, my friend, that is truly between you and the one who knit you together. It may be your sense of rejection or abandonment; it may be an addiction you've taken on to help you cope with your pain; it may be a mask you've been putting on so long you're almost fooling yourself. Whatever it is, I promise you that, if you simply ask God to reveal it to you, he will not hesitate.

Go to him now, won't you? Lay down your anger, your betrayal, your baggage, your pain. Lay down what you think you know about your family, your spouse, your friend, yourself. And please, I am begging you—lay down that image of who you long to be so that you may be all the Lord longs for you to be.

Until we are able to lay it down, we will never be able to function fully as the people God intended us to be. Admittedly, this is a tough assignment, but he doesn't ask us to do it alone. We can call on the supernatural power of the Holy Spirit to give us the strength. And we know that the God we serve doesn't just understand love; he *is* love.

In the space below, make a commitment to go forward in love. Write the name of a specific person or people whose hurtful actions you still carry with you. Then write all the emotions (anger, blame, bitterness, envy, etc.) you are laying down as well. Now reach out into glorious freedom—God is most certainly there to grab your hands.

I am forgiving _____ . (Use initials if you'd prefer.)

I am laying down my feelings of _____

_____

_____

_____

_____

_____

_____

Read Romans 8:9-11 again—out loud this time, as a prayer of praise. Thank God for the power he has given you through the Spirit to live as a more loving, forgiving, and whole human being. With his strength, you can break the chain!

> *God, thank you that I am no longer controlled by my sinful nature but by the Spirit because I have the Spirit of God living in me. I praise you that Christ is living within me, so even though my body will die because of sin, the Spirit gives me life because I have been made right with God. Thank you that the Spirit of God, who raised Jesus from the dead, lives in me. I know that just as you raised Christ Jesus from the dead, you will give life to my mortal body by this same Spirit living within me.*

Week 2

Introduction

Recommended Reading from *Named by God*: Chapters 4–7
Named by God Video Curriculum: DVD Session 2

This week we move from a panoramic view to a portrait view of the past. In week 1 we got a good grip on the sins that impacted our pasts—specifically, the ones we witnessed throughout our childhood and teen years. Last week was designed to get us ready for the hike we will climb together in the week ahead.

I know that for many of you, week 1 was difficult for one of two reasons: (1) the memories of the pain you endured in your childhood seem far too excruciating to walk through again, or (2) you come from a healthy home, and it may have been difficult to narrow down specific generational sins or negative examples.

If you find yourself in the first category, I want to encourage you that this is not just about dredging up old memories; there is a spiritual purpose behind it. And if you are in the second category, I pray that you hear my heart in this—in no way do I desire for you to dig up dirt that is not there. If there were no patterns of sin, hallelujah! Praise God for your family. I do, however, have every intention of encouraging each of you to get raw and vulnerable about where you have come from and what you have seen. It's called being real.

This week we continue the process of peeling back the layers of the past to reveal the core of who we are and what motivates our thoughts and actions in the present. If generational sin was the panoramic landscape of our journey, pinpointing the specific area(s) of suffering or consequences will be the portrait.

At this point, please allow me to offer a heartfelt warning. If you are committed to doing the work in this, there are two surefire things I can promise: (1) you will certainly be asked to relive some of your most tragic and painful past moments, and (2) by the end of this week you will be one step closer to feeling the fresh wind of liberty against your face like you have not known in years.

Week 2 is all about staring straight into the specific hurts that have been keeping you up at night and robbing you of peace and joy, as well as standing between you and the brilliant purposes God desires to reveal in your life.

Intro

Week 2

This is our theme passage for the week:

Never pay back evil with more evil. Do things in such a way that everyone can see you are honorable. Do all that you can to live in peace with everyone. Dear friends, never take revenge. Leave that to the righteous anger of God. For the Scriptures say, "I will take revenge; I will pay them back," says the LORD. Instead, "If your enemies are hungry, feed them. If they are thirsty, give them something to drink. In doing this, you will heap burning coals of shame on their heads." Don't let evil conquer you, but conquer evil by doing good. ROMANS 12:17-21

This passage is completely opposite of the way our culture trains us to react to those who offend, betray, or hurt us. As humans, we always default to our flesh if we take our eyes away from Jesus for even one moment. This is precisely why this week's study is a no-pass week! Don't skimp on the journaling, and don't skim the Scriptures we'll be discussing. We simply *must* trudge through this part of the journey together if we are going to get closer to being the people God intended us to be!

Group Session 2

This week we'll be talking about the human response to suffering that results from a collision with another human being. We will focus on the times when another person's sin leaves us staggering and speechless, the times when we have felt like victims. We will learn the biblical response when pain, heartache, and suffering are brought upon us.

You were running the race so well. Who has held you back from following the truth? It certainly isn't God, for he is the one who called you to freedom. GALATIANS 5:7-8

No one is righteous—not even one. No one is truly wise; no one is seeking God. All have turned away; all have become useless. No one does good, not a single one. ROMANS 3:10-12

1. It is not a matter of _____ a person will hurt you; it is a matter of _____ .

2. When a person hurts you, you have one of two choices:

1. Choose to _____ .

2. Choose to get _____ .

Bitter = afflicted; in misery; a wicked person in sin

3. Bitterness will completely block the _____ in your life, and it will keep you in the chains of _____ .

4. How do you know if you are bitter? You became bitter in one of three ways:

1. Another person sinned against you directly.

2. You *think* another person sinned against you directly (perceived sin).

3. You got jealous.

The words you speak come from the heart—that's what defiles you. For from the heart come evil thoughts, murder, adultery, all sexual immorality, theft, lying, and slander. MATTHEW 15:18-19

Whatever comes out of you exposes what was there.

5. The truth is, we are responsible for our own _____ .

"Don't sin by letting anger control you." Don't let the sun go down while you are still angry,
for anger gives a foothold to the devil. EPHESIANS 4:26-27

6. Satan wants you to blame everybody else besides yourself so that he can get a _____

_____ .

7. How do you deal with bitterness? Ask yourself, Do I want to be like _____

or _____ ?

Watch out that no poisonous root of bitterness grows up to trouble you, corrupting many.
HEBREWS 12:15

8. We must dig up the root of bitterness and _____ it!

Get rid of all bitterness, rage, anger, harsh words, and slander, as well as all types of evil behavior.
Instead, be kind to each other, tenderhearted, forgiving one another, just as God through Christ has
forgiven you. EPHESIANS 4:31-32

Your response cannot be contingent on the behavior of another person. Your response is only
contingent on what Jesus did for you.

Day 1

Not for the Faint of Heart

Begin today's study with prayer, asking God to reveal any areas of your past in which a person has sinned against you. Ask him to show you if there is someone you need to forgive or a hurt you need to allow God to heal. Are you letting another person's sin hold you back from full service and devotion to Christ? The wrong may have been done recently or a long time ago; it may have been committed against you or against someone you love deeply. Pray for the Holy Spirit to take over now and enable you to let go. Allow his guidance to set the cruise control on your life, and surrender to the gentle movement of God.

1. In the space below (or in a separate journal), write the name(s) of the particular person or people who have hurt you and the wrong(s) you're having trouble releasing from your grasp.

_____

_____

_____

_____

_____

_____

2. What emotions linger in your heart and mind from these past wounds?

_____

_____

_____

_____

_____

_____

3. We obviously won't be able to cover all the possible causes for being hurt, but the following list gives us a place to start. If any of these scenarios have been done to you, circle them. If you have done any of these to someone else, underline them. Be honest with yourself.

addiction	lying
adultery	rage
divorce	sexual abuse
gossip	stealing
hurtful words	verbal/emotional abuse
jealousy	withholding love

4. Read Job 1:6-12.

In verse 8, the Lord tells Satan to consider Job because he is _____ .

He is _____ . He fears _____ and stays

away from _____ .

5. Now read Job 1:13–2:8.

As you read, find the attacks Job faces, and list them below.

_____

_____

_____

_____

_____

_____

Job isn't just a fictional character in a story or some kind of symbol to prove a biblical point. He's a real person who endures more heartbreak than most of us will ever know. And because Job is a real man going through real issues, I believe he is vital to our own understanding of loss and pain. I believe one of the reasons Job suffers the way that he does is so you and I can better understand three things: who God is, who we are, and what God is working to accomplish in our lives.

Within a span of twenty-four hours Job goes from being one of the wealthiest men on earth to utter poverty. In total he loses five hundred teams of oxen, five hundred donkeys, three thousand camels, and seven thousand sheep. In one day he goes from having a household bustling with family to losing all ten of his children in a windstorm. And, as if this were not enough, not long after, Job's physical person is given over to an outbreak of inflamed sores that covers his body.

6. Take some time to journal about your most recent time of suffering. This can be any hurt, loss, or anguish you have recently experienced at the hands of another person. Don't worry whether other people would categorize it as a legitimate source of pain. If it is suffering to you, there is no big or small. Give a brief description of this time.

_____

_____

_____

_____

_____

_____

7. **As you recall this moment, answer the next question in complete honesty between you and God.**

Did you praise God in those very first moments of the aftermath of this event? (A simple yes or no will suffice.)

_____

8. **Now go back and reread Job 1:20-21.**

In verse 21, does Job curse or praise God in the aftermath of such unimaginable suffering?

_____

_____

What an awe-inspiring moment we get to eavesdrop on here! First, it is clear that Job is grief stricken over the pain he has endured—and may I interject that he should be. And so should you. Feeling the effects of another person's sin on your life *should* grieve your spirit. It is a natural part of being human, and God expects nothing less. When someone wounds us, we may get angry, we may weep, we may pace in circles for hours, replaying the event. Whatever the case for you, these are all normal, human reactions to pain at the hand of another. However, it is Job's *next* reaction that might easily be categorized as abnormal, or even absurd, by the majority of those who have been victimized.

Job worships.

As we read in Job 1:20-21, first, Job acknowledges that nothing was his to begin with. He honors God by recognizing that he is the same God who gives everything in the first place; therefore, he can rightly take it away. Second, Job owns up to his own frail and vulnerable condition as flesh—naked he came to this earth, and naked he will return. Nothing he acquires between his birth and his death will depart this earth alongside him. Finally, Job looks to the Lord and worships: "Praise the name of the Lord!" he says.

Now, think back once again to the account you chose to journal today.

Did you answer *yes* or *no* to the question after your recount?

9. **If you said yes, what impact did your response make on you and those around you in the days and weeks following the painful event?**

_____

_____

_____

_____

_____

_____

10. If you said no, at what point did you take the step to thank the Lord despite your pain? How would the turmoil have been different if you had taken it to him sooner rather than later? If you have yet to worship the Lord through your pain, what is holding you back from doing that?

_____

_____

_____

_____

_____

_____

As we conclude day 1 of this week, I can see no greater opportunity to worship the Lord. Do not allow your pain to stand in the way of knowing God more intimately. Pray that God will begin the often heart-wrenching, always humbling process of chiseling away your flesh, piece by piece, in order that you may clearly see his plan and purpose for your life.

As you pray, keep the following truth close to your heart: Satan can and will cause pain in the lives of God's children, but he can do so only with God's permission. And God will ultimately use that suffering to show his glory evermore radiant through your life as you come to a sweeter, richer sense of his love.

Day 2

The Whys of Life

Stay with me in this—we have only begun to scratch the surface of how to overcome the stumbling blocks of our pasts. This week we will continue to focus on the times when wrongs have been done against us, the times when we have had to play the role of victim while another human selfishly inflicted pain on us.

Take a few moments to close your eyes and block out every distraction around you. Lift your face to the heavens, and praise God for being in control, even when you feel out of control. Ask him to begin revealing himself to you in fresh ways, whether you are currently standing smack-dab in the center of a storm, healing from the aftermath, or rejoicing in a place of calm serenity.

> *If I have sinned, what have I done to you,*
> *   O watcher of all humanity?*
> *Why make me your target?*
> *   Am I a burden to you?*   JOB 7:20

Read Job 3—the entire chapter.

Despite this being a completely depressing read, did you happen to notice a recurring word from Job that has most certainly been uttered by your own mouth on more than one occasion?

That's right—the word *why*.

I absolutely adore the Lord for allowing this word into his holy Word, because it shows that he sees me in my time of need. He doesn't shy away from my questions, and he doesn't reprimand me for asking. He is like a patient parent with his young child. The questions may get repetitive and annoying, but he knows the child is going to be curious, so he lets his son or daughter ask.

In my lifetime I have learned that it is easy to ask God why but difficult to get a straight answer. As we learn from Job's life, there is nothing wrong with asking why, as long as we understand that God doesn't owe us the answer.

Questions We Ask in the Midst of Suffering about Ourselves

1. **Is God mad at me?**

Reread Job 7:20. Have you ever felt like you were God's target? Have you ever felt as though God were more of an enemy than your loving Father? Describe those experiences and feelings below.

_____

_____

_____

_____

_____

_____

_____

2. **Has God abandoned me?**

Read Job 16:6-11. Have you ever felt like God has turned his back on you? Have you felt as though he is no longer concerned about your well-being? Write those emotions and circumstances below.

_____

_____

_____

_____

_____

_____

_____

3. **What have I done to deserve this?**

Read Job 31:5-40. Have you ever come before God with a list of sins in order to have him show you which ones you're guilty of? Have you ever wondered what you could have done that would warrant such devastating suffering in your life? Document your reflections below.

_____

_____

_____

_____

_____

_____

_____

Questions We Ask in the Midst of Suffering about the One Who Hurt Us

4. **What was that person's motivation in hurting me?**

Read Job 30:10-13. Have you ever felt taken for granted by another individual and not known why he or she was treating you that way? Have you ever questioned the reason behind another person's choice to hurt you? Describe what that situation was like.

_____

_____

_____

_____

_____

_____

_____

5. **Will that person get what he or she deserves for hurting me?**

Read Job 34:10-11. Have you ever wanted someone who hurt you to be hurt in return? Have you ever desired someone to receive payback for the suffering he or she brought upon you? If so, document that moment below.

_____

_____

_____

_____

_____

_____

_____

God doesn't mind if we ask him questions amid our storms. Even Jesus asked his Father why he had abandoned him (see Matthew 27:46). But we need to be careful that we're not putting our focus on the answers instead of on God himself.

Think about it for a moment—does knowing why your arm is broken make the pain less intense or the arm less fractured? Nope! The knowledge of it only reaffirms the obvious. In the same way, knowing the why of your hurt doesn't heal your brokenness or ease your pain.

We must learn to depend on and lean on God's promise to be faithful to us, not on the unanswered questions of this life.

This leads us to a truth that may sound cliché but is no less true: God is in control! When it comes down to it, this is the only truth that gives us comfort in the midst of our suffering and consuming questions.

As we close, let's read Job 42:12-17.

Job's Blessings

6. List below the blessings God bestows on Job in the second half of his life.

_____

_____

_____

_____

_____

_____

_____

The purpose of this passage is not to assure you that every problem in your life will one day be solved or that all you've lost is guaranteed to be given back. The point is that, no matter what happens to you in this life, no matter how painful your situation may be, the Lord always has the final say!

I would like to leave you with one more glimpse of the sovereignty of God in all situations on earth, including your own. God not only knows of the suffering you have endured and will endure throughout your life, but he also gives you a warning so you can see it coming.

Scripture Matching

7. Read the following Scriptures, then draw a line to correctly match each to the truth contained in it.

Psalm 34:19	The world will bring troubles, but the victory has already been won.
Matthew 6:34	Each day will bring trouble, but you don't need to worry.
John 16:33	Even the righteous endure trouble, but only the Lord rescues.

As you end this time with the Lord, think back to Job. From an earthly perspective, his life may seem to be about losing everything only to receive the Lord's blessing in return. However, the most miraculous part of Job's story is not his suffering or his rewards but the remarkable opportunity he was given to know God more intimately through his trials. The Lord extends the same opportunity to us. Will you ask him now for eyes to see your pain as he does—as an opportunity to grow closer to him? Go to him now, and surrender your whys at his feet.

Day 3
....
Leave the Unknown Alone

Begin today's time of study with a moment of silence before your God. Ask him to place you in a hedge of protection from Satan as you read his living Word today. Ask him to bring to light any place of suffering that still lingers in your being and hinders you from your utmost service to him. Ask him to prepare you for any pain and tears these thoughts may ignite and to guide you to victory over your suffering—a victory he has already claimed for you.

Read Hebrews 12:1-11. Answer the following questions from your reading.

1. **Enduring life's struggles is compared to what in verse 1?**

_____

2. **Who has already endured the ultimate shame and opposition from sinful human beings?**

_____ (verses 2-3).

3. **When suffering comes our way, we are to endure its hardship as**

_____ (verse 7).

4. **God disciplines us because he is treating us as his** _____ (verse 8).

5. **If we accept our suffering and choose to grow from it, it will eventually produce a harvest of**

_____ (verse 11).

As humans, our natural tendency is to assume that only bad can come out of suffering. But God instructs us to have a different mind-set when we encounter hardship. There is a hidden blessing in it for those who accept it, for suffering is one of the most profound ways God chooses to let us know his heart on a deeper level.

As you think back to a specific season of hardship you have endured or are currently enduring, what would you say is your personal philosophy about pain and loss? The book of Job gives us three different perspectives on suffering from the key players throughout the story.

Views of Suffering from the Book of Job

Satan's View (Job 1:9-11)

People believe in God only when he is blessing them. If they face suffering, they will ultimately turn their backs on God.

The View of Eliphaz, Bildad, and Zophar (Job 5:7-8; 8:5-6; 11:11)

People endure suffering as a punishment from God for sin.

God's View (Job 42:2-6)

People endure suffering because God wants them to build their foundation on him, not on circumstances or other people. He wants to know that we will trust him in the bad times as well as the good.

6. **Which of these descriptions do you resonate with most? Circle one.**

Suffering results in denying God.

Suffering is punishment for our sin.

Suffering leads to trust in God.

God made creation to be perfect. The original world was a good and beautiful place where humans did not suffer. However, when sin entered the picture, so did corruption, conflict, pain, and ultimately, suffering. We cannot avoid suffering, but we do get some say in how we respond to it.

The Biblical View of Suffering

According to Scripture, there are five main causes for suffering. We will use David and his family as a case study for some of these causes of pain in our lives. The trials we go through come as a result of one (or more) of the following:

Our Own Sin (2 Samuel 12:13-14)

Suffering can come from our personal rebellion against the will of God. This is what happened to David as a result of his affair with Bathsheba. In cases like these, we are responsible for the suffering we experience as a result of our disobedience. (We will discuss this topic further in week 3.)

The Sin of Another Person (2 Samuel 13:12-14)

Suffering can take place in our lives because of the sinful actions of other people, as was the case for David's daughter Tamar. We can become victims of pain when others' ungodly choices seep into our lives.

Avoidable Disasters We Are Warned Of (Genesis 19:14-26)

As in the story of Lot and the destruction of Sodom and Gomorrah, we are sometimes warned with flashing red lights telling us to get out before we get hurt. God may use other people to sound the alarm, or he may advise us through his Word. Suffering comes when we refuse to heed the warning.

Unavoidable Disasters Brought On by God or Satan (Job 1:6-12)

Suffering can also be endured through circumstances that are simply out of our control—a serious illness, a devastating natural disaster, an economic crisis—anything brought into our lives that seems unexplainable. No human fault is involved, just a bold call for faith in the face of suffering.

The Result of Living in a Broken World (Romans 8:19-22)

Sometimes life is just that—*life*. Not a demonic attack or a divine revelation, just circumstances that knock us down when we least expect them. Sometimes the suffering we go through is simply a result of living in a fallen world. This creation is broken, and our bodies are broken. Ever wonder why you feel younger than you look? It's because, as a believer, your heart resides in heaven, while your body is left to age, wither, and deteriorate here on earth. Although everything that happens to you is allowed by God, not all of it is spiritual or supernatural.

7. **Read Paul's words in 2 Corinthians 12:7-10.**

   What does he say in verse 7 was given to keep him from becoming proud?

   _____

   How many times did Paul plead with God to take this away from him _____ (verse 8)?

   Write God's response to Paul's request in the space below (verse 9).

   _____
   _____
   _____
   _____

   Reread verse 10. Based on Paul's example, what should our response be in times of weakness?

   _____
   _____
   _____
   _____

In God's sovereignty and grace, he orchestrates healthy distributions of good and bad for us to encounter throughout our lives. In his wisdom, he knows that if we only experience blessings and constant protection from evil, we will go into our default mode—pride—and assume we have somehow earned those good things on our own merit. So God also allows suffering and burdens to intersect with the good, just as he did with one of his greatest servants, Paul. These trials keep us aware of our brokenness and encourage us to humbly surrender all before the one who holds our tomorrows.

Take some time to write down any unanswered questions that plague your mind as you think about your own suffering. As you write, ask God to give you the strength to leave those questions here on this page. As you turn to day 4, I beg you: do not bring them with you.

_____
_____

_____

_____

_____

_____

_____

_____

_____

_____

_____

_____

Suffering may enter your life for a variety of reasons: simply because you are human and your body is deteriorating or because you have made unwise choices and are feeling the aftermath of them or because God is using the trial as his chiseling instrument to make you more like his Son. Whatever the case, every scenario can be redeemed as an ultimate victory by the grace of God.

As we come to the end of our time together today, will you take a moment to meditate once more with the Lord? Ask God for the strength to draw continually on his abundant flow of grace so that he might turn your tragedy into his triumph. As you pray, keep this in mind: the Lord does not bestow his grace simply so we can get through the hard times. Ultimately, his desire is that we rise above and claim newfound meaning and purpose in the pain.

Day 4

The Portal to Power

Begin your time of study today by reading the following Scripture passage as a prayer. I encourage you to speak the verses out loud. Let the power of your voice resonate through the air and lift to the heavens as a sweet-smelling incense to your Father.

> *All praise to God, the Father of our Lord Jesus Christ. God is our merciful Father and the source of all comfort. He comforts us in all our troubles so that we can comfort others. When they are troubled, we will be able to give them the same comfort God has given us. For the more we suffer for Christ, the more God will shower us with his comfort through Christ.*   2 CORINTHIANS 1:3-5

On the following scale, place a mark where you feel you are today when it comes to suffering. Be honest with yourself.

1 ——————————————————— 5 ——————————————————— 10

1 = I am completely healed from the wrongs that have been committed against me in the past. I never dwell on the hurt done to me. It does not consume me, and I have given full forgiveness and love to the party who wronged me. He or she no longer plagues my thoughts or actions. I serve Christ on a daily basis as a fully restored and healed individual.

10 = I am consumed with suffering because of another person. I have been wronged in some way in the past, and it invades my thoughts, which in turn affects my actions. I am not able to serve God wholeheartedly because I don't feel restored enough to do so. I struggle with feelings of bitterness and anger toward the person who hurt me, and I would love nothing more than for this person to experience the pain he or she caused me.

I don't know about you, but I tend to cringe and sink a little lower in my seat whenever a pastor or teacher begins a message or lesson on forgiveness. To be honest, I have never particularly cared for others presuming they know my situation well enough to tell me I should forgive. For years I struggled with authentically forgiving the young man who raped me when I was fifteen. I also struggled to let go of the bitterness and anger I harbored toward my parents for getting a divorce. I have struggled to let go of plenty of smaller offenses, as well.

Now that I'm a teacher who has the precious honor of hearing other people's stories, I cry through an entire box of tissues with the insecure teenager who was sexually abused before she was old enough to know what sex was. I burn hot with anger as I hold the hands of a broken woman whose husband or boyfriend hurts her with his hands or his words. I breathe deep breaths of pain and compassion as I listen to countless stories of men and women who have been betrayed, abused, beaten down, and broken by another human being at some point in their lives.

For them, and perhaps for you, forgiveness seems, well . . . weak. It feels as though they are being asked to let the offender off the hook for the disgusting evil done against them. Precious one, I pray that you read this as though I were directly in front of you, looking straight into your eyes and squeezing your cheeks between the palms of my hands: *Forgiveness is not weakness. Forgiveness is the ultimate portal to power.*

The first step to opening the portal and finding the power to extend forgiveness, as well as to be freed from the chains of an unforgiving heart, is to allow God into that specific place of hurt.

As I counsel those who have endured excruciating blows from the hands of another, I find a recurring theme: most victims have never truly allowed God into their wounds. Many have allowed other "fixes" into their pain—they've attempted to mend that place of sorrow with relationships, stuff, addictions, or escape into a fantasy world. I've talked to numerous victims who have attempted to put a bandage on a deep laceration that is gushing blood and can only be treated with stitches.

Dear reader, we will now begin an exercise that I would walk through with you if we were sitting together in a one-on-one counseling session. We would both open our Bibles to Isaiah 53, and I would ask you to read the entire chapter aloud to me, slowly and clearly, pausing for breath between each phrase.

If you are in a spot right now where you can read this passage aloud, do so. If not, simply read it quietly and slowly to yourself, taking in each morsel of each phrase (don't forget the pauses).

1. Verse 3 calls Jesus "a man of _____ ."

2. Also in verse 3, what is Jesus "acquainted" or "familiar" with?

   _____

   _____

3. According to verse 4, what did Jesus take up or carry?

   _____

   _____

4. Why was Jesus tormented in this way (verse 5)?

   _____

   _____

5. How have we as humans responded to God's love (verse 6)?

   _____

   _____

6. Although Jesus would have had every right to protest his treatment, how did he respond (verse 7)?

_____

_____

7. Did Jesus deserve the pain and agony he endured (verses 8-9)?

_____

_____

8. Because of the death of Jesus, how will all wrongs against us one day be brought to justice (verses 11-12)?

_____

_____

As we close our time together for day 4, feel free to respond to the Spirit's movement within you however you feel led. Perhaps, like me, you may want to lay prostrate on the ground and weep before the Lord in gratitude for his love and grace. Perhaps you want to journal in more detail what you are thinking and feeling right now. Or perhaps you feel moved to pray aloud:

My Jesus, the Man of Sorrows, you bore the sin of my past, my present, and my future upon your back on the cross. You were rejected, despised, hated, and mocked for me. You had done no wrong, and yet you received the punishment for my wrong. How sinful I am, Lord, and how desperately I desire to be free from the chains of the memory of _____ [fill in with the specific name(s) of the one(s) who have hurt you or the specific hurt you have endured]. How deeply I long to release both this memory and myself from the clutches of my _____ [fill in with whatever emotions are being harbored deep within you, such as resentment or anger]. Lord, I realize that I have been covering this wound with _____ [fill in whatever person, substance, activity, or addiction you have used in an attempt to "fix" your problem]. I pray you will give me the strength to peel back the layers to this wound I have ignored and run away from for so long. I beg you for comfort as I allow your healing presence into this hurt place and surrender it completely to you. Although I may not feel peaceful, joyful, loving, or forgiving at this moment, I ask that the truth of your Word will overcome me and that I will act in that truth alone. Please give me peace of mind as I trust you, despite what I see or don't see, to bring justice to this evil against me. I leave this pain to be healed only by you, and I will do so again tomorrow, and the next day, and the next. In your healing name, amen.

Day 5

Access Code

Before we begin today, I should mention that this day will probably be bittersweet for many of us. It's bitter in that we will be asked to lay down our pride, and that is never easy. But it's also sweet in that to do so always—and I mean *always*—reaps great blessing from the hand of the Lord.

In week 2 we've focused on the areas in our lives where we've been the victims. My prayer is that through this week the Lord would bring us to a new place of release and healing from the wounds that have been inflicted upon us by another.

Before we get into our final day for the week, I encourage you to offer a sincere prayer to the Lord. Ask him for the ability to take a selfless look at your wound through the filter of the Cross. Whether your hurt stems from a parent, a friend, a spouse, a child, a stranger, or the hand of God himself, I beg you to pray for the courage to get through this study today. I assure you—you are going to need it!

1. Let's begin our day by writing 1 Peter 4:8 in the space below. (Don't skip this part!)

_____

_____

_____

_____

_____

_____

2. Now write out Romans 12:21.

_____

_____

_____

_____

_____

_____

Although it is healthy to pinpoint the specific places of hurt in our lives and go through the process of forgiving those wrongs, God wants more than that from us. His Word tells us that we're not only to extend love and forgiveness in the cataclysmic moments but also to have a constant posture of forgiveness through the everyday ins and outs of life.

By asking you to love your enemy, God is not minimizing or downplaying your hurt. He is simply saying, "Let the authorities handle this one."

Have you ever been in a situation, big or little, where a person was in the wrong but you had to let it go and allow someone else to handle it? For example, maybe when you were a kid, your classmate cheated off your paper. You were mad, but the teacher had to handle it. Or when you were a teenager, perhaps a bully at school made fun of you. You were hurt, but your parents had to take care of it. What about at work? Maybe a coworker plays solitaire on her computer all day instead of getting her job done. You are frustrated because more work falls on you, but ultimately your boss has to handle it. Perhaps a criminal has wronged you and you'd like to take justice into your own hands, but you realize you need to let the legal system run its course.

3. **Now document a personal example from your own life.**

_____

_____

_____

_____

_____

_____

_____

_____

_____

_____

_____

Forgiveness isn't about waving the white flag of surrender or dismissing the situation; it is simply about appealing our case to a higher court and leaving it to those who have the power to bring about justice. God isn't saying that when someone does us wrong we should just let it go. He's not asking us to lie down and let evil win. He's saying that when someone harms us, our best course of action is to surrender ourselves to the sovereign God, who is big enough to do something about it.

4. **Draw a line from the Scripture verse to its matching description of God's forgiveness.**

Isaiah 43:25	removes the memory of our sin
Matthew 26:28	blots out our sin
Isaiah 55:7	brings healing
Jeremiah 31:34	free and generous
1 Peter 2:24	poured out for many

5. **Place a check next to the aspects of forgiveness that you find difficult to grant.**

_____ never again remembering the sin

_____ blotting out the offense

_____ being healed from the offense

_____ pardoning the person for his or her wrongdoing

_____ pouring out forgiveness on the one who sinned

Read Luke 17:1-4. Jesus didn't place the anguish of this world onto his bloodied and broken back so that *you* would spend your life walking around bloodied and broken. You simply cannot hold on to an offense that Jesus Christ has already willingly carried for you. As long as you do, you are giving your offender the opportunity to hit you over and over again.

However, as you choose to act out of love and forgiveness, you begin to set the captive free—and surprisingly, you just may realize that captive was you. Forgiving the one who hurt you means refusing to be held in chains by what someone else has done to you.

Does letting God take the reins in this area sound impossible, unimaginable, or unbearable to you right now? Yeah, I've been there too. But the glorious truth about this forgiveness thing is that we don't go it alone. In fact, we *can't* go it alone. I assure you, I have spent countless hours expending sideways energy in an attempt to forgive someone out of my own strength. If this is where you find yourself, may I offer a tender word of wisdom here: don't be stupid! Once we get to the place of surrendering our wounds to Jesus, we are left with only one clear and workable option—use *his* power, not our own!

Let's take a few moments for an in-depth look at a man named Asa, a king of Judah who knew he needed a little help. Let's see what God does with a man who is humble enough to call out for supernatural power.

6. **Read 2 Chronicles 14:11. Who does King Asa say he trusts in?**

_____

_____

7. **Now read verse 12.**

What does the Lord do to King Asa's enemies?

_____

_____

8. **Read 2 Chronicles 15:1-2.**

What does Azariah tell King Asa in verse 2? Who will stay with Asa?

_____

_____

9. Write down the names of the people you need to forgive. What tangible steps do you need to take to make that happen?

_____

_____

_____

_____

_____

_____

_____

_____

As we wrap up this week of study, keep in mind that forgiveness begins with an action, not an attitude. If you are waiting for the *feeling* of forgiveness to come upon you, you will likely be waiting for a long time. The beautiful truth is that in Christ you do not have to wait—you have the access code of love and the power of the Holy Spirit at your constant disposal. You just need to use them!

As you close this time in prayer, honestly reflect on where your heart is with the Lord. After spending a moment in meditation with him, complete the exercise below.

10. Place a check next to each step you have sensed God accomplishing in you this week.

_____ I allowed God into my hurt.

_____ I identified with Christ in his suffering.

_____ I put my trust in God to bring justice.

_____ I was able to grant forgiveness.

_____ I was able to extend love.

_____ I cried out to God for power.

Part II: Transforming Your Present

Week 3

Introduction

Recommended Reading from Named by God: Chapters 8–10
Named by God Video Curriculum: DVD Session 3

If you study the book of Jonah (tucked away toward the end of the Old Testament between Obadiah and Micah), you will find a captivating account of a man who received a direct message from the Lord and chose to disobey him.

Although you may have grown up believing the story of Jonah was just about a big fish, that is far from the point. Jonah's story is me. Jonah's story is you. Jonah's story is the story of all those who know what they are supposed to do and instead run in the opposite direction.

God calls Jonah to preach in a wicked city called Nineveh (the capital of Assyria), with a population of more than 120,000 people. God comes to Jonah and tells him to go there, but Jonah hops on a boat that literally takes him in the opposite direction—to a city called Tarshish.

While Jonah's on the boat, a violent storm overtakes the sea, and the other passengers realize something isn't right—that somewhere along the way they've picked up a bad apple, so to speak. By this point, Jonah is in such a deep depression for his rebellion that he plans out his own death by asking the crew to just throw him overboard and be done with it.

Here's where the story gets good, right? Enter . . . the big fish.

So God prepares this giant fish to swallow Jonah. Although the fish tends to always get the spotlight in this account, the true attention should go to the fact that the Lord *provided* the fish to protect his chosen instrument Jonah. In a supernatural act of mercy, Jonah later gets vomited onto dry land (gross!) after asking for the Lord's forgiveness. He preaches to the city of Nineveh, and as a result, the entire city turns from their wicked ways and places their trust in the Lord. In Jonah 3:10 we read that the people are so sorrowful over their past sins that the Lord actually changes his mind. Instead of destroying Nineveh as planned, the Lord spares the city and everyone within it. (Wow—did you realize your brokenness and surrendered prayer before the Lord can work to change his mind? Pretty powerful stuff!)

Great story, right? Well, wait just one minute before you do your happy-ending dance. You see, although Jonah asks the Lord for forgiveness, there is still this nasty feeling somewhere deep inside him. Here he has seen firsthand the Lord's plan for him, experienced his protection, and tasted his mercy. Plus, God used him to lead an entire city to the truth! But dear old Jonah still isn't a happy camper.

Jonah has yet to surrender himself completely to the Lord. He is still choosing his own ways over the Lord's ways. Even after all he's been through, Jonah still lacks faith. Jonah hasn't embraced that deep-level trust in which, despite what he can and cannot see, he will believe God simply on the fact that he is *God*—the Creator of the universe who sees the landscape from eternity to eternity.

Apparently Jonah doesn't think these Assyrians—longtime enemies of his people—deserve to be saved. So when the Lord doesn't go through with his original plan to wipe them out, Jonah 4:1 tells us that Jonah is downright angry.

Jonah throws himself a pity party and begins to wallow and complain. He goes so far as to beg the Lord to take his life rather than let him sit by and watch the people of Nineveh receive forgiveness for their sinful past. Jonah plants down his pitiful self and pouts for a while, just stewing on all the forms of punishment he feels the city should have had coming. But all the while he should have been contemplating the sins within his own heart that needed to be dealt with!

Have you been there? I know I have. I've folded my arms defiantly across my chest, with all the maturity of a three-year-old, just waiting for someone to get what he or she deserved instead of owning up to my own pride and sin.

As we embark on week 3 of our journey together, I invite you to humbly ask the Lord the following questions:

In what ways am I rebelling and acting like Jonah?
In what areas am I running the other direction instead of following your call?
What sin in my own heart am I overlooking as I focus on other people's sins?

Jonah serves as a powerful warning to all of us. He may have lived thousands of years ago, but we make the same mistakes he made. We ignore the warning signs, flirt with the wrong attitudes, and turn to our plans instead of to God's.

This week we will take time to look at the attitudes and behaviors that drive a wedge between us and God. We will examine ways we are not the victims but the offenders. And just so we are all clear, I will not sugarcoat this by referring to it as anything less than what it is—sin. I will not call it our "mistakes" or our "weaknesses" or our "issues." The Word of God is black and white about sin, and the sooner we quit playing around in the gray zone, the sooner we will experience the full-throttle power of the Lord on our lives!

It's time to stop treating the symptoms. Instead, we are going straight to the source of the infection.

Group Session 3

This week is all about identifying the areas that God has clearly cut off yet we continue to attempt to resuscitate. These may be particular seasons of our lives, certain dreams, relationships, addictions, thought processes, habits, or ways of seeing ourselves (guilty, condemned, unattractive, unqualified, insecure). This week we will learn the steps of daily living as those who put to death earthly desires and live in the power of the resurrected Christ.

Let's read Colossians 3:1-10.

1. There are two competing realities that you, as a believer, will deal with on a daily basis:

Your _____ is alive and well.

Your _____ is out to kill you.

2. What is the solution for living daily outside of the chains of sin? To _____

_____ **to the life that is already yours in Jesus Christ.**

Heart: represents your _____

Mind: represents your _____

Is the life that you are living worthy of the death that Jesus died?
Now let's read Romans 7:14-22.

Do not let sin control the way you live; do not give in to sinful desires. Do not let any part of your body become an instrument of evil to serve sin. Instead, give yourselves completely to God, for you were dead, but now you have new life. So use your whole body as an instrument to do what is right for the glory of God. Sin is no longer your master, for you no longer live under the requirements of the law. Instead, you live under the freedom of God's grace. ROMANS 6:12-14

3. Nothing in your life is going to change as long as you are only _____

your sin. You must _____ it out of your life!

4. You cannot do God's will _____ .

5. Ask yourself this question: Is there a sin in my life right now that I am struggling to kill off?

6. The most _____ sins in your life are

   1. The ones you do not know are there but are there.

   2. The ones you have yet to confess.

7. Ask yourself this question: Is there a place I am continuing to mourn when God has rejected it?

If we are continuing to pursue a place God has rejected, we are in _____

because we are not in the _____ of God.

Now the LORD said to Samuel, "You have mourned long enough for Saul. I have rejected him as king of Israel, so fill your flask with olive oil and go to Bethlehem. Find a man named Jesse who lives there, for I have selected one of his sons to be my king."   1 SAMUEL 16:1

8. Two things God is saying to anyone who is holding on to something old instead of embracing something new:

_____ and _____

Day 1

The Devouring Lion

Child of God, your enemy, the devil, wants nothing more than to feed you a pack of lies to persuade you that you aren't worthy of communicating with the Lord Almighty. Satan uses every past sin and every weak spot to make you feel ashamed, dirty, and of no value to your heavenly Father. As we spend this week getting a better grasp on what Satan is up to, I have no doubt that the enemy will be furious with our attempts to gain insight into his evil schemes.

Take this moment to ask God to cage that roaring lion—to block him from setting foot into your time with the Lord today. Prepare for an intense week by humbling yourself before the Lord in prayer. Praise God right now for his indescribable power. Remember that, although Satan may be the prince of this world, you serve a God who is King over life, death, and eternity!

Today we'll begin by establishing a foundation about our adversary, the devil. I hope you're up for a little pop quiz! Let's test your knowledge about who Satan is, how he came to be, and how much power he has.

1. **Circle the correct answers below.**

(1) Satan "fell" from . . .
   a) a throne
   b) heaven
   c) a mountaintop

(2) Prior to his fall, Satan was . . .
   a) a saint
   b) a demon
   c) an angel

(3) Satan's given name, Lucifer, translates to . . .
   a) morning star
   b) evil one
   c) roaring lion

(4) Satan became evil when he . . .
   a) gathered a bunch of demons to help him perfect his evil villainous laugh
   b) got a red cape and a pitchfork
   c) desired the throne of God for himself

(Although you aren't being graded, here are the correct answers: 1 = B; 2 = C; 3 = A; 4 = C. See Isaiah 14:12-22.)

Prior to his pride-induced fall from grace, Satan was an angel. Yes, that's right—an angel. In fact, Satan was not your ordinary angel. He stood in the presence of the Almighty as one of his most highly ranked angels. We know this because Isaiah 14 tells us he was given the name Lucifer, which means "morning star." The name literally translates as "light bearer." Lucifer was not only an angel residing in the courts of God Almighty; he radiated beauty beyond compare. He was exquisite.

2. **Read Isaiah 14:12-15.**

In your own words, write Lucifer's intended plan (pay close attention to verses 13-14).

_____

_____

_____

_____

3. **Now read Proverbs 16:18, and fill in the blanks below.**

_____ goes before destruction, and haughtiness

before a _____ .

The key to understanding how Satan came to be has everything to do with these two words: *pride* and *fall*. Lucifer wanted to capture the throne of God for himself and, in turn, to receive all the worship.

4. **In Revelation 22:16, who else is referred to as the "bright morning star"?**

_____

5. **How does Jesus fulfill this title in a way that Satan never could?**

_____

_____

_____

Our God is a loving and compassionate God, a God of second chances. But he will not tolerate his glory being imitated or hijacked in any way. All worship and honor belong to God, and he will not allow that to be compromised.

> *The devil took [Jesus] to a very high mountain and showed him all the kingdoms of the world and their splendor. "All this I will give you," [Satan] said, "if you will bow down and worship me." Jesus said to him, "Away from me, Satan! For it is written: 'Worship the Lord your God, and serve him only.'"*
> MATTHEW 4:8-10 (NIV)

When Lucifer fell from the courtyard of heaven, he brought along not only a certain amount of power but a few fellow stragglers as well. These "fallen angels" are otherwise known as demons. They were undoubtedly allies with Lucifer as he crafted his plan to take over the heavenly throne. But when God Almighty sensed the prideful longing dwelling within the heart of Lucifer, he cast him and his followers out of his presence. Lucifer and his companions hit planet Earth and have been running around wreaking worldwide havoc ever since!

To say that Lucifer was angry when his plan to take over heavenly worship failed is an understatement.

6. **Read John 12:31.**

Satan is the current _____ of this world but will one day be cast out.

7. **Read 2 Timothy 2:22-26. Fill in these blanks using the last part of verse 26.**

Those who oppose the truth have been _____ by the devil to do whatever he wants.

8. **Read 1 Peter 5:8.**

What truths can we take from this verse?
Satan is continually looking for his next victim. He roams this earth, never sleeping, constantly prowling for easy prey.
Satan is ferocious. Like a roaring lion, he and his demons are on the hunt for blood.
Satan desires your life—not only in a spiritual sense, but in a physical sense as well.

9. **Read John 8:44.**

This verse states that Satan is the father of what?

_____

10. **Read the following Scripture passage out loud.**

Be strong in the Lord and in his mighty power. Put on all of God's armor so that you will be able to stand firm against all strategies of the devil. For we are not fighting against flesh-and-blood enemies, but against evil rulers and authorities of the unseen world, against mighty powers in this dark world, and against evil spirits in the heavenly places. Therefore, put on every piece of God's armor so you will be able to resist the enemy in the time of evil. Then after the battle you will still be standing firm.

EPHESIANS 6:10-13

I realize we have just gone through a crash course on the background of Satan. Perhaps you are saying to yourself, *I thought this study was about my relationship with Jesus. Why study up on the devil?* And it is precisely this question that can get us into a big, heaping mess of trouble.

Throughout this week we will ask God to reveal to us the pieces of our own flesh that are driving a wedge between us and our Creator. We absolutely must begin our discussion on this topic by addressing the enemy. You see, if we give in to any part of our flesh, in big or small ways, we open the door for Satan and his companions to wreak havoc in our lives . . . and in the lives of those around us.

Our dishonesty, anger, foul language, unforgiving spirits, gossip, pride, or misguided passions can be used by the enemy to destroy us. Any sin we harbor in our hearts and minds will inevitably result in a "come get it" holler for Satan.

As we close our lesson today, I encourage you to offer a prayer to the Lord. I beg you to take this time seriously. Investigating the hurt we inflict on ourselves and others can be downright brutal, and we need the Lord's help.

Whether you've been sensitive to the supernatural forces around you for some time or whether this idea of Satan as an active force is new territory for you, know that the evil one has developed a strategy to destroy you—and he is not afraid to use it. He will do everything he can to keep you from growing during this week of study. The enemy would very much enjoy watching you fill your head with knowledge and then wooing you into a state of complacency to keep that head knowledge from sinking deep within your heart and your actions.

Will you close now with a battle prayer? Ask God to break you and humble you. Pray against the enemy and all his attempts to sabotage you. I will see you tomorrow on the battlefield, my friend!

Day 2

A Prime Target

Let's begin today by arming ourselves against the attack of the enemy and against our own pride. Pray right now for the Lord's protection. Feel free to claim the following verse as your armor before proceeding:

You belong to God, my dear children. . . . The Spirit who lives in you is greater than the spirit who lives in the world.
1 John 4:4

Today we will be walking through a bit more self-assessment as it relates to how well you know your enemy. Work through the questions below in all honesty before the Lord.

1. When you think of someone who is a prime target for an attack of Satan, what type of person comes to mind?

_____ a lost loner—someone who has yet to receive salvation and doesn't seem to care about God

_____ a saved slacker—someone who has received salvation but doesn't live a life that exemplifies godly character

_____ a passionate pursuer—someone who has received salvation and is a devoted follower of Christ

Although all people, believers and unbelievers alike, are susceptible to the crafty web Satan spins, most church-going, Bible-toting, Scripture-quoting Christians are shocked to learn that Satan's scope is set directly on *them*, the devoted followers of Christ.

Why?

Because Satan's beef is not with the mere mortals of this world; he is fighting mad at the omnipotent Lord God. And, because Satan is powerless before God and unable to attack him directly, he goes after the next best thing—God's children.

2. Read 2 Corinthians 11:3.

Does this verse seem to be describing an enemy of God or a child of God? (Circle one.)
enemy   child

What two adjectives are used to describe the devotion of this person who is so easily corrupted by the enemy?

_____ and _____

3. According to Scripture, Satan has several plans of attack laid out for the believer. Read each passage below, and match it to the corresponding truth:

2 Corinthians 2:10-11   Satan can corrupt the believer's devotion to Christ.

2 Corinthians 11:3   Satan can torment the believer spiritually and physically.

2 Corinthians 12:7   Without the help of Christ, Satan can outwit the believer.

Now let's take a moment to talk about Satan's plan of attack for the unbeliever.

4. Read Matthew 24:4-14.

What warning does Christ give in verse 4?

Don't let anyone _____ you.

According to verse 10, who (or what) will people turn away from?

_____

According to verse 12, the love of most will grow cold because of what?

_____

As we get real before the throne of God this week, I must come to you with my own confession. I have been a child of God for twenty years now, and during that time I have been struck by many arrows from Satan's bow. I praise God for the times I called on his mighty power and wisdom to block the sharp edges from penetrating my life. But I shamefully regret the times I found myself tangled in a web of sin spun by Satan and intended for me.

I regret that reaching my breaking point of surrender to the Lord took this hardheaded, pride-filled diva far longer than it should have! There was obvious sin in my life that I should have recognized, called out, and pleaded forgiveness for. But those sins were more like the fever than the infection—symptoms of something darker, deadlier, and more dangerous that lurked deep within my soul. It wasn't until I admitted I was powerless to change on my own that I started getting somewhere.

Maybe you are in a similar place. God has a mission and purpose for your life, but unless you come before him daily in confession and surrender, you are postponing this breathtaking adventure.

Close in prayer now, admitting to God that you cannot change on your own and that you need him to change you from the inside out.

Day 3

....

The Warning Signs

Begin this day of study in prayer, asking God to break your heart about any areas of sin in your life that you are currently struggling with. Perhaps you are entering today's study time a little unsure of what is keeping you from feeling complete in Christ. You may not be able to pinpoint an exact sin, but you know that your relationship with Christ is not functioning at full capacity. If that describes you, pray right now for God to reveal the exact action (or inaction) that is keeping you from wholehearted devotion to him.

> *Brothers and sisters, if another believer is overcome by some sin, you who are godly should gently and humbly help that person back onto the right path. And be careful not to fall into the same temptation yourself.*
>
> GALATIANS 6:1

By this point we have established a working knowledge of our enemy. Not only do we have a solid grasp on who Satan is, but we also have a better understanding of those he seeks to attack. Now that we are more aware of Satan's power, it is vital to spend our time today uncovering the art of satanic seduction.

1. **Read Matthew 3:16–4:1.**

   In verse 16 we find out that Jesus has just been _____ .

   What does God the Father say about Jesus (verse 17)?

   _____

   _____

   Circle the word *then* at the beginning of Matthew 4:1.

   Almost immediately after his baptism, Christ undergoes a direct attack from Satan in which he is led to the desert for what purpose?

   _____

   _____

It may surprise you to discover that most Christians are not in a period of open rebellion when the enemy throws them a curveball. On a personal level, I can say that I tripped over the largest stumbling block of my life right after a time of being on a spiritual high with my Lord. Satan loves to take a season of closeness with the Lord and catch the believer off guard with his attack. Satan's lie to us goes something like this: "Sure, you're holy enough, you go to church enough, you serve in ministry enough—you don't need to worry about a demonic attack. I would never mess with you! Just keep rockin' and rollin' in ministry. . . . You got this thing!"

2. Have you ever experienced a time of temptation from the enemy after a high point in your Christian walk? If so, describe that experience below.

_____

_____

_____

_____

_____

_____

_____

_____

_____

_____

_____

_____

3. Read 2 Thessalonians 2:3-7.

What word is used to describe Satan's power of lawlessness in verse 7?

_____

Satan almost always attacks the believer's mind. Why? Because the mind is the place where God communicates with us and reveals himself to us. What we believe in our minds soon leads to the way we act. Therefore, it is critical that we daily renew and refresh our minds through God's Word. If we neglect this discipline, we leave ourselves vulnerable to the captivating lies of Satan.

The deceived will soon find themselves deceiving. If Satan can get you to believe his lie, then he can get you to tell a lie. And thus begins the downward spiral to destruction.

4. Can you think of a time when you allowed a secret area in your life to cause you to lie to others? If so, describe what happened below.

_____

_____

_____

_____

_____
_____
_____
_____
_____
_____
_____
_____

5. Read Isaiah 64:6.

When we are unclean, we shrivel up like a leaf, and our sins _____
_____ like the wind.

Apart from a clear, set course of following God, we are like leaves being tossed back and forth by the wind. And it is in this place of flailing about that Satan likes to hold us captive. Satan desperately desires to keep us ignorant of God's will and movement in our lives. If Satan can keep us busy in ministry, busy at home, busy at work, busy at school, or hung up with other drama, then God's voice can soon be drowned out. We start to doubt that God is speaking to us at all.

6. Read Hebrews 12:1.

Sin promises to make our lives easier, but what does it really do?

_____
_____

One of the weights that tends to slow us down in our journey of faith is impatience. We want to rush God into action, and as a result we become restless, worried, fearful, and anxious about the what-ifs and whys in this life. When this kind of thinking takes over, we can be sure we are not fully trusting in the sovereign God to do what he is so great at doing—being God.

7. Have you ever found yourself caught in a web of sin because you got tired of waiting on God and took matters into your own hands? If so, describe that moment below.

_____
_____
_____
_____
_____
_____
_____

_____

_____

_____

_____

The destroyer targets the believer's mind, body, will, and heart. He sees an area of sin in your life and seizes it to keep you far from God. Just to bring it home, here are some sample game plans of the deceiver so you'll recognize them when they invade your life.

Satan's Strategies

Sin: You lose your cool easily with difficult people in your life.
Satan's plan: To hinder your witness for Christ.

Sin: You look at your coworker or friend who is not your spouse in a lustful way.
Satan's plan: To lead you into infidelity.

Sin: You sleep with that guy before marriage.
Satan's plan: To keep you stuck in that sin and disqualify you from a God-glorifying marriage.

Sin: You use your words to bash your spouse, friend, or family member.
Satan's plan: To create dissension and stress in your life.

Sin: You stay in bed because you don't want to face the day.
Satan's plan: To lead you into the bondage of depression.

And the list could go on.

8. **Read Revelation 2:1-7. What does it mean to stay true to your first love?**

_____

_____

_____

_____

9. **Where are you right now in your relationship with your first love? Be real about your struggles— it's just you and the Lord. Record the areas of sin that are drawing you into Satan's big old web and pushing you further from the light of your Redeemer.**

_____

_____

_____

_____

_____

_____

_____

_____

_____

_____

_____

_____

Let's close by praying the following passage as a claim of victory as well as a daily commitment to the Lord. As you read these verses, circle every action you intend to do from this moment forward.

A final word: Be strong in the Lord and in his mighty power. Put on all of God's armor so that you will be able to stand firm against all strategies of the devil. For we are not fighting against flesh-and-blood enemies, but against evil rulers and authorities of the unseen world, against mighty powers in this dark world, and against evil spirits in the heavenly places. Therefore, put on every piece of God's armor so you will be able to resist the enemy in the time of evil. Then after the battle you will still be standing firm. Stand your ground, putting on the belt of truth and the body armor of God's righteousness. For shoes, put on the peace that comes from the Good News so that you will be fully prepared. In addition to all of these, hold up the shield of faith to stop the fiery arrows of the devil. Put on salvation as your helmet, and take the sword of the Spirit, which is the word of God. Pray in the Spirit at all times and on every occasion. Stay alert and be persistent in your prayers for all believers everywhere.   EPHESIANS 6:10-18

Day 4

Cleansing Confession

This High Priest of ours understands our weaknesses, for he faced all of the same testings we do, yet he did not sin. So let us come boldly to the throne of our gracious God. There we will receive his mercy, and we will find grace to help us when we need it most.   Hebrews 4:15-16

As we begin our time in God's Word today, I encourage you to breathe in this beautiful passage of Scripture. We will use this passage to light our way as we head down the path of healing and restoration from any strongholds that hold us captive.

I don't know about you, but I am greatly comforted by the fact that my Lord not only knows about my weaknesses but has personally come in direct contact with the same temptations. Because of Christ's sacrifice, we have been given the right and the privilege to come before his throne with complete confidence. Doesn't that thrill your heart? We are not to come before the Almighty cowering in fear but in great boldness. And we come knowing we will receive grace and mercy! Praise God today for these two precious gifts that you and I do not deserve yet are given so freely.

So as you come before the Lord right now, approach his throne in all confidence. Kneel before him, if you feel led. Lift your hands to the sky. For today, do not close your eyes, but instead lift your face to the heavens with the certainty that you will receive God's grace and mercy. Do not cower behind your sin, your weaknesses, or your mistakes. Do not allow the enemy any space in this time with your Lord. We are going to break those chains today!

1. Write 1 John 3:9 below.

_____

_____

_____

_____

_____

_____

2. **Now record the first reactions that came to your mind as you read this passage.**

_____

_____

_____

_____

If you are anything like me, this is where you force down a huge lump that has been gathering in your throat as you have been reading. Satan is always working to get us to sit in the "time-out" chair of guilt. He even twists the Word of God in an attempt to bring hopelessness instead of transformation. He wants us to question everything we believe to be true about God and our status as his children: _Oh no, I thought I was really a Christian! But if I'm a true Christian, how can I keep doing this?_

I'd like to pause here to ask you to muster up all the courage you've got to name the sin in your life right now. Bring it into the light and confess it to God. What habitual sin keeps holding you back? Is it looking at pornography, losing your temper, cheating on your taxes, exaggerating your stories, lying to your spouse, cheating on your spouse, having sex with your boyfriend, gossiping with your friends?

Now fill in the blank below. Go ahead—check over your shoulder if you need to. There's no one but you and God.

3. **If I am a true Christ follower, how is it that I keep on . . .**

_____

_____

_____

_____

It's important to realize that, once you become a believer in Jesus Christ, God does not eradicate your old sinful nature. Instead, God imparts to you a _new_ nature, giving you a desire for spiritual, holy things. But you still have to do battle against your sinful self.

Perhaps this is a helpful way to understand 1 John 3:9: true-blue, for-real children of God do not habitually and deliberately sin, for they have a new nature planted within them that is incapable of sinning. Oh yes, children of God are tempted to sin and sometimes fall (or jump) right into it. But eventually God in his mercy breaks through to them in the form of sorrow, guilt, shame, or conviction.

4. **Read 2 Corinthians 7:10-11.**

What type of sorrow brings repentance?

_____

_____

_____

_____

What is the difference between godly sorrow and worldly sorrow?

_____

_____

_____

_____

List the attributes (based on verse 11) that are produced in believers when they surrender to godly sorrow.

_____

_____

_____

_____

5. Okay, it's time for a little self-evaluation. In what areas of your life are you putting your little toe in the water of temptation? What seemingly innocent activity in your life could, with time, grow into a full-blown addiction?

_____

_____

_____

_____

6. In what areas of your life are you feeling convicted? What step can you take today to start heeding that conviction?

_____

_____

_____

_____

7. If there is currently a pattern of sin in your life, put a check mark beside the description that best matches your experience.

_____ I feel a prick that is frustrating me.

_____ I feel a sting that is causing guilt.

_____ I feel a stab that is causing me to suffer.

8. Conviction isn't just about _feeling_ guilty—it's about acknowledging the truth of what God says is right and wrong, regardless of what our emotions tell us. Take a moment now to think, not feel. Journal below what you are thinking in regard to your sinful state.

_____

_____

_____
_____
_____
_____
_____
_____
_____
_____
_____

9. **Read Psalm 51:17.**

What kind of sacrifice pleases the Lord most?

_____
_____
_____
_____

10. **Read 1 Samuel 16:7.**

What does God look at as he is choosing the people who will serve him?

_____
_____

11. **Read Galatians 6:1.**

According to this verse, how should fellow believers be restored from their sin?

_____
_____

12. **Read 2 Corinthians 2:6-8.**

God does not want us to be overcome with discouragement over our sin. Instead, he calls believers to _____ and _____ those who have sinned (verse 7).

13. **Read Proverbs 29:25.**

Do you find yourself spending more time and energy trying to please people than pleasing God? Give an example of a time when this has happened.

_____
_____

_____

_____

_____

_____

_____

_____

_____

_____

14. **Read Psalm 56:3-4.**

What emotion is taken care of when you place your trust in God instead of people?

_____

_____

15. **Read 1 John 2:1-2.**

What does Christ do in our defense when we sin?

_____

_____

16. **Read Hebrews 10:19-23.**

What kind of hearts do we need in order to enter the presence of God (verse 22)?

_____

_____

What kind of attitude can we have as we enter God's presence (verse 22)?

_____

_____

If we come before the throne of Christ boldly, what does verse 22 say will be cleaned?

_____

_____

17. **Tell about a time you let one of your fears (for example, fear of consequences, fear of what people might think or say, fear that God would not be there to catch you) hold you back from true repentance. How would you handle that situation differently in the future?**

_____

_____

_____

_____

_____

_____

_____

_____

_____

_____

As we come to the end of day 4, can you say honestly that you have surrendered everything to the Lord? Let's close by reading the following quote. As you read, confess your failures before him.

> Confession is a difficult Discipline for us because we all too often view the believing community as a fellowship of saints before we see it as a fellowship of sinners. We feel that everyone else has advanced so far into holiness that we are isolated and alone in our sin. We cannot bear to reveal our failures and shortcomings to others. . . . Therefore, we hide ourselves from one another and live in veiled lies and hypocrisy. . . . We are sinners together. In acts of mutual confession we release the power that heals. Our humanity is no longer denied, but transformed. [2]
>
> RICHARD J. FOSTER

[2] Richard J. Foster, *Celebration of Discipline* (New York: HarperCollins Publishers, 1978), 145–46.

Day 5

A Joyful Return

As you begin today, pray in humility and in admiration of your Creator. Praise him for the grace-filled blood he shed for your sins—past, present, and future. When Christ was nailed to the cross, his blood paid for not only the sins you've already committed but also the sins you *will* commit. You are covered and cleansed through and through! Now ask God to give you the power to believe him and to let your life reflect this truth.

Welcome to your journey home!

The story we are going to talk about today is a familiar one, but there is no better way to conclude this section on overcoming our pasts. If you have read or heard it numerous times before, I pray it will fall fresh on your heart today.

Week 3   Day 5

1. **Read Luke 15:11-32.**

Instead of staying at home with his family, the younger brother packs all his things and moves to a _____ (verse 13).

After spending the entirety of his inheritance, Little Brother finds himself working for someone who sends him out to do what (verse 15)?

_____

The prodigal son (by the way, *prodigal* means "wasted") finds himself so starved for food that he longs to eat what (verse 16)?

_____

2. **Have you ever attempted to "find yourself" apart from the guidance of God? If so, what did that season look like? What were your plans? Where did you run?**

_____

_____

_____

_____

_____

_____

_____

_____

3. Verses 17-19 state that the young man finally decides to do what?

_____

_____

4. Have you ever been so homesick for the loving embrace of your Lord that you completely stopped what you were doing and instantly broke into a full-speed run toward home? What happened, and what finally caused you to wake up?

_____

_____

_____

_____

_____

_____

_____

_____

5. Read the first part of verse 20 again. The father sees his son coming while he is still

_____

Verse 20 says the father is filled with what toward his son?

_____

When the son returns home, does his father rebuke him or rejoice with him?

_____

I love this next part.

6. What does the end of verse 24 say the household begins to do upon the son's return?

_____

7. Who is mentioned in verse 28?

_____

_____

8. **Big Brother is . . .**

_____ happy

_____ indifferent

_____ mad

Oh, siblings! They can cause such drama. But the character of the older brother isn't thrown into this story to depict a prime example of sibling rivalry. God gives us this detail to remind us what to expect of people made of flesh. Verse 28 tells us the older brother flat-out refuses to go to the party. Oh, the fun he surely misses by not going inside to celebrate!

As disheartening as it may be, inevitably there are those people who simply refuse to join your transformation party. Those people may come in the form of disappointed family members, betrayed friends, or confused onlookers. When your secret sin hits the light of day, prepare yourself for those who want no part in your return celebration. These people are just a little bitter that God is celebrating you rather than condemning you. They falsely believe they have done something to deserve the love of the Father (see verses 29-30).

9. **Write verse 32 below.**

_____

_____

_____

_____

_____

_____

As you peel back the layers of your own rebellious ways, undoubtedly there are those of you who are thinking, *But I have prayed, I have begged, I have pleaded for forgiveness, yet I still feel tainted and unworthy. I still feel captive to my flesh. I know I'm accepted as a child of my Father, but I still feel like a prodigal.*

Oh, honey, have I been there!

Here are some biblical truths I've discovered along the way to speak to those feelings:

- There is a big difference between forgiveness and repentance. Forgiveness happens the moment we accept Christ (see 1 John 2:12); repentance is the recurring act of being released from the grief of our sin (see 2 Corinthians 7:9). You will never receive true healing and release from your sin until you repent—until you make a complete 180-degree turn away from the sin and refuse to look back. You may ask for forgiveness, and the Lord is certainly faithful to forgive. But until you turn away from the sin completely, you will never feel right with God.

- There is a big difference between the Lord's forgiving you and your accepting that forgiveness. The Bible promises, "If we confess our sins to him, he is faithful and just to forgive us our sins and to cleanse us from all wickedness" (1 John 1:9). The truth is, the Lord may forgive you all day long, but until you choose to believe him, you will never be free.

- There is a big difference between a clean slate and a wiped-out memory. The Lord is faithful to forgive us of all unrighteousness, but he does not cause us to forget what happened, and he doesn't eradicate the consequences of our sinful actions. The purpose of memory is to remind us not of our wretched state but of God's grace, love, and mercy in bringing us out of the pit. Our memories also remind us just how awful it was being down in that dark hole so that we might never venture into it again (see James 1:24-25).

- There is a big difference between guilt that leads to godly sorrow and guilt that leads to condemnation. The healthy kind of guilt (otherwise known as conviction) rushes over you after you disobey the Lord. This guilt, which comes directly from the Holy Spirit, is healing in nature and lasts only until you repent of the sin. On the other hand, the guilt that leads to condemnation is directly from the hand of Satan. Demonic guilt is unproductive and keeps you bogged down long after you've repented. This guilt will beat you down, tell you how unworthy you are of God's love, and make you feel wretched. (A note of warning here: other Christians may misguidedly use this form of guilt to make you feel bad about your sin. But this is the work of Satan, not the voice of the Redeemer!)

As we close this week, I pray—oh, how I pray—that you have found yourself in a big, humble heap of brokenness. Remember, God is attracted to messes, for it is only when we are broken in surrender that he has room to show up and work. As we will learn in the weeks to come, there is no greater thrill and pleasure than being smack-dab in the center of God's will.

Don't give the enemy one more foothold in your life. Don't go one more day accepting false guilt and shame for sins God has already forgiven. Commit to trusting God despite what Satan or others say.

Let's conclude this week by reading aloud the following passages from the Psalms:

*Oh, what joy for those
    whose disobedience is forgiven,
    whose sin is put out of sight!*   PSALM 32:1

*Finally, I confessed all my sins to you
    and stopped trying to hide my guilt.
I said to myself, "I will confess my rebellion to the LORD."
    And you forgave me! All my guilt is gone.*   PSALM 32:5

*Though we are overwhelmed by our sins,
    you forgive them all.*   PSALM 65:3

*You forgave the guilt of your people—
    yes, you covered all their sins.*   PSALM 85:2

*He forgives all my sins
    and heals all my diseases.
He redeems me from death
    and crowns me with love and tender mercies.
He fills my life with good things.
    My youth is renewed like the eagle's!*   PSALM 103:3-5

Week 4

Introduction

Recommended Reading from *Named by God*: Chapters 11–13
Named by God Video Curriculum: DVD Session 4

If you can live by the following two principles, I will go so far as to say that, regardless of what happens *to* you, God will be so great *in* you that each day will be the best of your life. These foundational realities are the theme for week 4.

- Before God formed you, he knew you. You are divinely knit together.
- Before God formed you, he set you apart for a specific purpose. You are called to a divine destiny.

I believe with all my heart that if we would allow these truths to seep deep into our pores, we would fall so in love with Christ that we would live each moment of our present free from worry, doubt, insecurity, anxiety, depression, bitterness, jealousy, and fear.

As we approach week 4, I pray that each of us would gain a new perspective on who we are in Christ—that there is a purpose and identity so intimately written upon our souls that, no matter how far we have veered from it, God is more than capable of realigning our lives to it.

The point is not that we could ever be deserving enough, worthy enough, smart enough, religious enough, or good enough. The point is that none of that determines our identity.

My prayer for you this week is that God will bring you to a place where you can step into your destiny—not because God overlooks your sin or because you have somehow lived a good enough life to deserve it, but because Christ has paid the price to make that possible.

I should warn you, though—this is a lot easier said than done. There's no time to waste— let's get going!

Group Session 4

You made all the delicate, inner parts of my body
*   and knit me together in my mother's womb.*
Thank you for making me so wonderfully complex!
*   Your workmanship is marvelous—how well I know it.*
You watched me as I was being formed in utter seclusion,
*   as I was woven together in the dark of the womb.*
You saw me before I was born.
*   Every day of my life was recorded in your book.*
Every moment was laid out before a single day had passed.   Psalm 139:13-16

As the Lord's children, we are destined for things beyond our wildest dreams. Yet we can waste years—or even a lifetime—missing out on our God-given potential if we give in to self-defeating and self-debilitating mind-sets.

This week we will take a look at how God reveals his plan to us and how we can make sure we don't count ourselves out of that plan before we ever have a chance to experience it.

1. We often talk about how wonderful God is, but we greatly _____ **his design.**

2. How you feel about yourself is a direct _____ **about how you feel about God.**

God always works from the inside out.

Even before he made the world, God loved us and chose us in Christ to be holy and without fault in his eyes. God decided in advance to adopt us into his own family by bringing us to himself through Jesus Christ. This is what he wanted to do, and it gave him great pleasure. So we praise God for the glorious grace he has poured out on us who belong to his dear Son.   Ephesians 1:4-6

3. You cannot truly worship and sense his presence in your life until you can place
_____ on what he has made.

Embrace _____ .

4. Stop just believing _____ God and begin _____ God.

Day 1

The Wave of Doubt

Let's begin our study by spending some time alone with our God. Whether you currently find yourself sipping a cup of coffee as the sun breaks through the window or sitting beside a small nightstand lamp just before bedtime, I want to remind you that God is the all-consuming light. Wherever light abides, darkness cannot remain; it is simply impossible.

Allow God's light to whisper his message into your ear in this moment, keeping Satan's darkness from penetrating this sacred time. As part of your prayer time, read Psalm 139 out loud. You may whisper it to the Lord, weep it to him amid tears of gratitude, or simply claim this verse with a tone of victory.

You have searched me, LORD,
*   and you know me.*
You know when I sit and when I rise;
*   you perceive my thoughts from afar.*
You discern my going out and my lying down;
*   you are familiar with all my ways.*
Before a word is on my tongue
*   you, LORD, know it completely.*
You hem me in behind and before,
*   and you lay your hand upon me.*
Such knowledge is too wonderful for me,
*   too lofty for me to attain.*

Where can I go from your Spirit?
*   Where can I flee from your presence?*
If I go up to the heavens, you are there;
*   if I make my bed in the depths, you are there.*
If I rise on the wings of the dawn,
*   if I settle on the far side of the sea,*
even there your hand will guide me,
*   your right hand will hold me fast.*
If I say, "Surely the darkness will hide me
*   and the light become night around me,"*

even the darkness will not be dark to you;
    the night will shine like the day,
    for darkness is as light to you.

For you created my inmost being;
    you knit me together in my mother's womb.
I praise you because I am fearfully and wonderfully made;
    your works are wonderful,
    I know that full well.
My frame was not hidden from you
    when I was made in the secret place,
    when I was woven together in the depths of the earth.
Your eyes saw my unformed body;
    all the days ordained for me were written in your book
    before one of them came to be.
How precious to me are your thoughts, God!
    How vast is the sum of them!
Were I to count them,
    they would outnumber the grains of sand—
    when I awake, I am still with you.

If only you, God, would slay the wicked!
    Away from me, you who are bloodthirsty!
They speak of you with evil intent;
    your adversaries misuse your name.
Do I not hate those who hate you, LORD,
    and abhor those who are in rebellion against you?
I have nothing but hatred for them;
    I count them my enemies.
Search me, God, and know my heart;
    test me and know my anxious thoughts.
See if there is any offensive way in me,
    and lead me in the way everlasting. (NIV)

1. **As you read through this psalm, what parts did you find easy to claim and what parts did you find difficult to claim at this point in your faith journey? Make a list below.**

Easy   Difficult

_____   _____

_____   _____

_____   _____

_____   _____

_____   _____

_____   _____

_____   _____

2. Journal about the moments when you most strongly feel self-doubt creeping in or when you tend to question your self-worth.

_____

_____

_____

_____

_____

_____

_____

_____

_____

_____

3. As you read Psalm 139, what truths spoke to your doubts? What does it say about who God is and about who you are?

_____

_____

_____

_____

_____

_____

4. Place a check by the thoughts that most often plague you. (Mark all that apply.)

_____ No one would ever want to be with someone who has a past like mine.

_____ I can't stand the way I look! I am so ugly.

_____ I don't think I'm good enough to do this job.

_____ I am a horrible parent. I don't do enough for my kids.

_____ Maybe I am good for nothing, like he said.

_____ I'm too fat, and no one will ever find me attractive.

_____ I just can't seem to do anything right!

_____ I'll never be enough for him, so I might as well leave.

_____ He will never be enough for me, so I might as well leave.

_____ I would love to pursue that path, but everyone will think I'm a joke.

_____ I am not talented enough to do that.

_____ I am not skilled enough to do that.

_____ I am not attractive enough to do that.

_____ I am not worthy enough to have that.

_____ I am not good enough to overcome that.

5. **Why do we find ourselves doubting who God made us to be? This problem has been around since literally the beginning of time. To get some background on this, read Genesis 3:1-6.**

Who comes along and in verse 4 plants seeds of doubt in Eve's mind?

_____

List the three ways Eve justifies her sin in verse 6.

The tree was _____ .

The fruit looked _____ .

She wanted the _____ it would give her.

If Satan can cause us to doubt God's will for us, then he can keep us in a holding pattern of justifying our own plans and missing out on God's blessings. The inevitable consequence will be bad decisions, which lead to sinful activities, which tragically result in encouraging others to engage in sinful behavior as well.

Christians who continue to justify their sin will not grow to their full potential, nor will they accomplish the purposes God has set them apart to fulfill.

6. **Read James 1:6-8.**

Write the entire passage in your own words.

_____

_____

_____

_____

_____

_____

What is a doubter or a person with divided loyalty compared to (verse 6)?

_____

What is the end result for this type of person (verse 7)?

_____

Satan is always going to bring up this question to us: "Does God really care about you?" Those who vacillate, replaying the question in their minds but never fully embracing the truth, are like a wave on the sea. Verse 8 calls this type of person unstable and "divided." The original Greek literally means "a person of two minds or two souls." We can't wholeheartedly trust in God while also trusting in something else, such as the flesh or this world.

The greatest struggle we will ever face in terms of doubt is our doubt that we have worth to the Lord. I can't tell you how many times I've thought God was pretty much done with me.

I have messed up way too many times—I just don't deserve his blessing on my life.
I have chosen my own way for far too long—I doubt God has enough grace and blessing left for me.
There's no point in changing my ways—God gave up on me a long time ago.

But the Bible has another way of looking at things.

7. Read Ephesians 1:4.

Based on this verse, do you have anything to do with being chosen or called? (Circle one.)

Yes　　No

8. Read Colossians 1:16.

Fill in the last part of this verse.

Everything was created _____ .

9. Finally, read Romans 8:28-30.

Whose purpose have you been created for and called to?

_____

_____

Based on this passage, do your works, your church attendance, your good behavior have anything to do with God's value of your life? (Circle one.)

Yes　　No

Perhaps you doubt your value and worth to God today. But the Word of God is clear—before you ever showed up on the scene, God's plan was in place, and it was bigger than all your problems. God's sovereign will for your life overcomes all your insufficiencies.

As we close our time in God's Word today, let's go to him in prayer, offering up all our doubts, our failures, and our disappointments. Ask God that you might be overwhelmed with his truth, not others' opinions. Ask him to give you the strength to be constant in him—no longer drifting like a wave on the sea, but filled with a steady trust in him despite your circumstance.

Day 2
....
He Is Delighted

Once you begin to let go of your doubts and truly believe that the way God designed and created you was completely intentional, the concept of his love is a little easier to grasp. Begin your time of study with a prayer of praise. Reflect on the verse below, and repeat the words aloud if you feel led. Thank God for creating you, and praise him for being worthy to receive all the glory and honor.

> *You are worthy, O Lord our God,*
> *to receive glory and honor and power.*
> *For you created all things,*
> *and they exist because you created what you pleased.* REVELATION 4:11

For day 2 of our study this week, I feel it absolutely necessary that you leave this time with an understanding of how much the Lord loves you and delights in you. In order for you to transform your present, you must grasp how much you are worth to your heavenly Father. (Side note: I am referring to your worth, not in the eyes of other people or yourself, but in the loving eyes of the Lord. Big difference!)

In order for us to fully grasp God's love for us, it's necessary to bring God's character a little closer to home. So many people I speak with tend to view God as the old man sitting on a throne, ready to launch a bolt of lightning at anyone who looks like he or she is even thinking about getting into trouble. Although many give lip service to acknowledging that he is a God of love, deep in their hearts they believe that God primarily acts out of wrath.

The truth is, God experiences a full range of emotions. When Jesus lived on the earth, he personally felt the entire gamut of human emotions, and the Bible describes God the Father and the Holy Spirit experiencing the same feelings you and I do.

1. **Draw a line from the Scripture to the corresponding emotion.**

Exodus 20:5	joy
2 Kings 22:13	jealousy
Nehemiah 8:10	sorrow/grief
Psalm 86:15	anger
Ephesians 4:30	compassion

When we lose sight of the true nature of God as he relates to his children, we also lose sight of our purpose and identity. The more we view God as aloof and unapproachable, the more we view ourselves as unworthy of his blessing and a relationship with him.

2. Do you sometimes feel small in God's eyes? What are some areas in your life in which you feel too small to accomplish God's purposes?

_____
_____
_____
_____
_____
_____
_____
_____
_____
_____
_____
_____

The Lord desires us and delights in us. However, as we discovered in the passages above, he is also a jealous and angry God who grieves over the sinful choices we make. But his emotions are never tainted with selfishness or sin; he feels this way because he knows those decisions will only bring us heartache.

3. Just as the Lord delights in us, each of us should make it our heart's desire to delight and please him. Read the Scripture verses listed below. Underneath each one, document the attributes of a person who is pleasing to the Lord.

Psalm 147:11
_____
_____

Psalm 149:4
_____
_____

Proverbs 15:8-9
_____
_____

Romans 12:1
_____
_____

2 Corinthians 5:9

_____

_____

Colossians 1:10-12

_____

_____

4. In the list above, what attributes are you pursuing on a daily basis?

_____

_____

_____

_____

_____

_____

_____

_____

5. What attributes are currently lacking in your life and need to be worked on?

_____

_____

_____

_____

_____

_____

_____

_____

6. What are some specific steps you can take to pursue those qualities each day?

_____

_____

_____

_____

_____

_____

_____

_____

Our desire to please God is not the same as our desire to please our parents, our spouses, or our bosses. In these efforts, we work to please others so we might find favor in their eyes. In our relationship with God, we know that, although God recognizes and blesses holy living, no amount of work could ever be enough to earn his favor. This purpose of pleasing the Lord is not about us; it's about bringing worship and glory to him. "The time is coming—indeed it's here now—when true worshipers will worship the Father in spirit and in truth. The Father is looking for those who will worship him that way" (John 4:23).

Notice in this verse that it is God who is doing the searching here. In our own strength, we are incapable of worshiping the Lord or pleasing him. It is the Lord who seeks us out and enables us to worship and please him by the power of the Holy Spirit. Worship is the human reaction to divine intervention. We must never assume that worship is *our* worship, for it is only possible if our loving God inclines our hearts toward him.

7. **Read Isaiah 29:13.**

While the people's mouths offer words of praise to God, their _____ are far from him.

8. **If you are a churchgoing girl (which is something we should all aspire to be), list some of the reasons you attend church.**

_____

_____

_____

_____

_____

_____

_____

_____

In any of the above blanks, did you happen to write something like, "Because the Lord has been gracious enough to stir in my spirit the desire to worship him in community"? Romans 14:6-8 encourages us to view every move we make as an opportunity to worship and honor God. But Scripture also instructs us to set aside special time for corporate worship. Hebrews 10:25 says, "Let us not neglect our meeting together, as some people do." God created us to be in community with one another, and he intends for his people to find joy in coming together as a body to worship him.

As we close our time in prayer, meditate for a moment on how mighty God is and how small we are. Think in big-picture terms here—the Lord doesn't need us to make him any more God than he is. In fact, if left to our devices, we can't think of even one act that would please him. However, through the sinless sacrifice of his Son, Jesus, God's wrath has been satisfied. His heart longs to include his children in his Kingdom purposes.

Praise his mighty name now.

Day 3

The Payoff of Promises

Begin today's time of study in prayer, banishing the enemy from your thoughts and preparing your heart for what the Lord desires to show you. I challenge you not to come before the Word of God as if this were just another day. Child of God, this is a new day—a day he has chosen to give you life and breath. A day he desires to smile on you and delight in you. A day in which, if you allow him to, he just may rock your world. Come before his throne with expectation and a grateful heart.

We spent day 2 of this week researching some ways the Bible says we can please the Lord and give glory to him. Today we'll focus on God's plan of good for our lives, using this passage as our guide:

> *God is so rich in mercy, and he loved us so much, that even though we were dead because of our sins, he gave us life when he raised Christ from the dead. (It is only by God's grace that you have been saved!) For he raised us from the dead along with Christ and seated us with him in the heavenly realms because we are united with Christ Jesus. So God can point to us in all future ages as examples of the incredible wealth of his grace and kindness toward us, as shown in all he has done for us who are united with Christ Jesus. God saved you by his grace when you believed. And you can't take credit for this; it is a gift from God. Salvation is not a reward for the good things we have done, so none of us can boast about it. For we are God's masterpiece. He has created us anew in Christ Jesus, so we can do the good things he planned for us long ago.* EPHESIANS 2:4-10

Today we'll dive into the true account of a man named Joseph to show how God works to fulfill the promises he has given us.

Let's begin by reading Genesis 37:5-11.

Joseph is only seventeen years old when God starts giving him a vision for his life. What he doesn't realize at that young age is that it's not always wise to openly share the dreams and passions we feel God has given us. Most often there is still much work to be done in our own lives before those dreams can be fulfilled, and chances are God needs to empty us of our pride first.

Before we talk about the specific dreams God has for us as individuals, we need to delve into the promises he makes that hold true for all his children. Let's look at a few of those now.

1. Circle the promises given in each of the following passages.

Each of you must repent of your sins and turn to God, and be baptized in the name of Jesus Christ for the forgiveness of your sins. Then you will receive the gift of the Holy Spirit. This promise is to you, and to your children, and even to the Gentiles—all who have been called by the Lord our God.

ACTS 2:38-39

Since we have been made right in God's sight by faith, we have peace with God because of what Jesus Christ our Lord has done for us. Because of our faith, Christ has brought us into this place of undeserved privilege where we now stand, and we confidently and joyfully look forward to sharing God's glory.

ROMANS 5:1-2

"I will be your Father, and you will be my sons and daughters, says the LORD Almighty." Because we have these promises, dear friends, let us cleanse ourselves from everything that can defile our body or spirit. And let us work toward complete holiness because we fear God.

2 CORINTHIANS 6:18–7:1

The Scriptures declare that we are all prisoners of sin, so we receive God's promise of freedom only by believing in Jesus Christ.

GALATIANS 3:22

His divine power has granted to us all things that pertain to life and godliness, through the knowledge of him who called us to his own glory and excellence, by which he has granted to us his precious and very great promises, so that through them you may become partakers of the divine nature, having escaped from the corruption that is in the world because of sinful desire.

2 PETER 1:3-4 (ESV)

In addition to these rich, universal promises, God has also given *you* a personal, intimate vision for your life—a plan that is specific to you as an individual. I can't help but wonder as I write, *What dreams has he given to you? What unique promises has he made to you that he has impressed on your heart?* Maybe he has given you a vision for a certain relationship you should invest in, a particular service opportunity you should pursue, a business you should start, a place you should go, or a person you should speak to.

2. What specific dream or vision has God given you for your future? Document that in detail here.

_____

_____

_____

_____

_____

_____

_____

_____

_____

_____

3. **What pieces of this dream will be difficult for others (your spouse, your friends, your family members) to understand and support?**

_____

_____

_____

_____

_____

_____

_____

_____

Now let's fast-forward thirteen years in Joseph's life and read Genesis 42:6-25.

Thirteen years after Joseph first started getting revelations of God's vision for his life, there's a glimpse into the payoff of God's promise to Joseph. After enduring many hardships, Joseph is now second-in-command in the most powerful nation in the world. It is here that he starts to see God's dream finally coming to fruition.

4. **Skip ahead and read Genesis 50:20.**

What do you think God wants to teach us through the story of Joseph?

_____

_____

_____

_____

One of the lessons that is evident from Joseph's life is that God always fulfills his promises. But I'd also like to take a look at the *way* in which the Lord fulfilled his promise to Joseph.

Many of us tend to lose sight of God's goodness, faithfulness, and delight in us because we lose sight of the process. We focus on the end result, expecting God to bring about the fulfillment smoothly and instantly. We fail to recognize that a delay between the promise and its fulfillment doesn't mean God is slow or has forgotten about us. The process is the point!

We often cling to stories about people who ask God for something and receive immediate gratification. Our culture is driven by success and reward, and we are drawn into captivating tales that reinforce such a worldview.

However, after all I have been through, I have come to one revolutionary—and I believe biblically accurate—conclusion. It is not only the promise of God that shows his goodness; it is also the fact that he allows us to go through the process with him. The Bible is full of heroes, such as Moses, Joseph, David, Joshua, and Daniel, who were shaped into greatness through the process of walking the hills and valleys with the Lord.

I admit that it can be easy to lose sight of what God is doing when the time frame for his promises feels longer than we expected. Maybe you've been there:

You've been longing for a baby for years, but all your pregnancies have ended in miscarriages.
You've been praying for your wayward son for a decade, but he is still on drugs.
You've been looking for a job for a year, but nothing seems to pan out.
You've been a bridesmaid in countless weddings but still haven't had a wedding of your own.
You've spent the past several months begging God for healing, but your loved one is only
    getting worse.

5. **In what ways have you lost sight of the dream God has given you as you've waited for his dream and his timing?**

_____
_____
_____
_____
_____
_____
_____
_____
_____

6. **What are some specific ways you've been able to see God working through the process in this situation? What have you learned about him, others, or yourself as you've waited for his unique promise to unfold in your life?**

_____
_____
_____
_____
_____
_____
_____
_____
_____

I will tell you from personal experience that my entire life changed when I began embracing the process rather than the payoff. Instead of spending all my time searching for the answer, the reward, the paycheck, the next thrill, I began breathing in the beautiful (and often gut-wrenching) steps along God's path. God is with you each moment, waiting for you to see him for who he truly is—not just as a God who can move mountains and part waters, but as a God of the little things too.

Day 4

Time to Grow Up

Begin today's study in prayer, asking the Lord to grant you supernatural wisdom and discernment as you open his Word. Ask him to reveal to you any areas of spiritual immaturity in your life. Ask God to give you the strength to pursue him on a daily basis.

> *We will no longer be immature like children. We won't be tossed and blown about by every wind of new teaching. We will not be influenced when people try to trick us with lies so clever they sound like the truth.*
>
> EPHESIANS 4:14

1. In the space below, list an area in your life where you feel you have extensive knowledge—in other words, a field in which you are mature. This could be a hobby, a career, an area of study, or an aspect of Christian life.

_____

_____

_____

_____

_____

2. When it comes to this area of expertise, what personal strides have you taken to bring you to this level of maturity (for example, learning from a mentor, taking classes, attending workshops, making daily investments in this activity, etc.)?

_____

_____

_____

_____

_____

_____

3. **What are some of the life plans or dreams you've had at various points in your life? Which have been realized and which haven't? How do these plans compare to God's plans for you?**

_____

_____

_____

_____

_____

_____

_____

_____

In a society inundated with instant gratification and superficiality, the idea of growing up in our relationship with Jesus can easily get pushed aside. We are so accustomed to living in the fast lane—hitting the drive-through for a quick meal, handing the cashier a tiny piece of plastic to pay for our purchases, rushing from one thing to the next on our overcommitted schedules. If we're not intentional about it, other things will crowd out our spiritual growth.

Maturing in our faith is not just for preachers, seminary professors, or the intellectually gifted. We must not succumb to the lie that, if we've been Christians long enough or if we attend church frequently enough, we will somehow arrive and it will no longer be necessary for us to grow in our faith. Scripture tells us this is a dangerous place to be: "My beloved, as you have always obeyed, so now, not only as in my presence but much more in my absence, work out your own salvation with fear and trembling" (Philippians 2:12, ESV).

Take special note of the phrasing "work out your own salvation." In other words, keep going, keep moving, keep grinding. Don't stop!

In order to get to this place of maturity with the Lord, we need to commit ourselves to the avid pursuit of one thing—wisdom.

4. **Read James 1:5.**

What does this verse say you must do to gain wisdom?

_____

_____

_____

_____

And how will it be given to you?

_____

_____

_____

_____

5. List the ways you are currently pursuing godly wisdom on a week-to-week basis.

_____

_____

_____

_____

_____

_____

_____

_____

To help you, here are the top five questions I ask myself to assess where I am in my maturing process with the Lord:

- Am I spending time daily reading God's Word?

- Am I intentionally memorizing Scripture each week?

- When there is a decision to be made, do I turn first to God's Word before getting advice from friends or family members?

- Is the Word of God becoming more satisfying to me? Do I delight in God's Word more than food, sleep, sex, and any other thrill this life has to offer?

- Am I getting better at discerning when Satan is deceiving me? Am I getting better at discerning when God is calling me?

6. After assessing your current commitment to spiritual growth, document below which of these five areas you need to spend some time working on.

_____

_____

_____

_____

_____

_____

_____

According to Romans 12:2, we are transformed when our thoughts are transformed! Not by going to church more, not by hanging out with our friends more, and certainly not by watching more television. Total transformation starts in the one place we receive information, discern truth, and make decisions—our minds.

As we close our time in God's Word today, let's meditate on the following verse and then close in prayer before him.

Dear brothers and sisters, one final thing. Fix your thoughts on what is true, and honorable, and right, and pure, and lovely, and admirable. Think about things that are excellent and worthy of praise. Keep putting into practice all you learned and received from me—everything you heard from me and saw me doing. Then the God of peace will be with you. PHILIPPIANS 4:8-9

As you pray, ask the Lord to transform your mind and help you fix your thoughts on him. Ask him to grant you the strength you need to spend time in his Word . . . until it becomes something you simply cannot live without!

Day 5

Complete Transformation

Let's begin our time together before the Lord in prayer. When you look in the mirror, you might not readily describe yourself as beautiful, but I assure you, child of the Almighty, that you are *exquisite* according to your Father. He created your outside and is pleased with the way you look, but he is even more concerned with your inner appearance. Instead of focusing on being externally beautiful, let's pray for God to make us "glory-ful"!

1. **Read Romans 12:2.**

   Let God transform you into a new person by _____ .

2. **Read Philippians 3:19.**

   List the things on the minds of the people described in this verse.

   _____

   _____

   _____

   _____

   _____

   _____

3. **Place a mark next to the statement that most accurately depicts where you are spiritually at this point in your life.**

   _____ I rarely pray or read my Bible.

   _____ When time allows, I get a few words in with God.

   _____ I spend a few moments with God almost daily.

   _____ I spend time reading and meditating on God's Word every day.

4. **Read Colossians 3:1-4.**

According to these verses, what should you think about?

_____

_____

_____

_____

5. **Read Matthew 4:4.**

What should people live on rather than just food?

_____

_____

_____

_____

6. **Read Acts 20:32.**

What can the Word of God, or "the message of his grace," do for you?

_____

_____

_____

_____

7. **Read 2 Timothy 3:16-17.**

List everything Scripture is useful for.

_____

_____

_____

_____

_____

Now that we understand transformation begins in the mind, how do we go about changing our thought patterns? It is important to remember that our minds are constantly bringing in information, and they give priority to what we bring in most often and what we concentrate on most intensely.

As we continue in these patterns over time, our minds create habits—those default places our thoughts go to without any effort. If we desire to break a certain habit, we must give our minds a new priority—a new habit to replace the old one. In other words, if we want transformation, we're going to have to be intentional about it!

8. **Draw an arrow from the word you feel currently describes you to the word you would like to replace it with in the future. (Repeat this for any words on this list that apply to you.)**

lazy	loving
insecure	joyful
arrogant	humble
angry	healed
bitter	positive
jealous	loving
intimidated	confident
anxious	encouraging
fearful	wise
worried	faithful
addicted	patient
critical	kind
condescending	free
foolish	selfless
withdrawn	motivated
lifeless	outgoing

I pray the above exercise helped you pinpoint a few of the places in your life in need of transformation. I encourage you to take a few moments now to ask God to show you one specific area to focus on first. Then, with that in mind, we'll look at three steps necessary for mind renewal. If you truly desire to change, you must be intentional about each one of these steps.

1)   Repetition

If you decided to take part in your first marathon, I doubt you'd simply show up on the day of the race and take off. No—that would be a disaster. Instead, you would start your training and preparation months before the actual event. You might get on a treadmill on day one and make it only five minutes before you start huffing and puffing. However, if you make running a priority each day, you gradually create a new habit. Ingrained habits are formed through repetition, and thus they change behavior. All the while you are getting better, and before you know it, you are running thirty minutes instead of five.

9. **List three things you do out of habit. These are behaviors you take part in almost automatically each day, sometimes without thinking.**

_____

_____

_____

What spiritual habits could you add to your life?

_____

_____

_____

2) Concentration

The world we live in inundates us with so many distractions that concentration is becoming a rare commodity. Think about it: is there a time in your day when you are alone in complete silence, with no people talking, no radio or TV on in the background, no phone beeping—just you focusing on a specific thing? It's hard to do, isn't it?

And it's not just distractions from the outside that get us sidetracked—our minds are constantly buzzing with internal noise too. It's only when we intentionally concentrate on something and quiet the noise around us and in us that we can center our minds on what's really important.

10. **What are three major distractions that keep you from concentrating on God's Word? (Let's focus on things that aren't really necessary in our lives, such as television, computer, texting, etc.)**

_____

_____

_____

3) Reflection

Reflection involves taking things one step further—from quieting our minds to actually changing our internal reality. This step is so often overlooked, but true change isn't possible unless we are willing to revolutionize the way we see our situations and ourselves.

Let's say that I want to break the unhealthy cycle of self-defeating thoughts. First, I take time to read God's Word every day (that's repetition). As I do, I concentrate. I make it a point to get alone in quiet and read God's Word without distraction. But let's say I stop there. Sure, I might begin to come out of my funk for a few days or even weeks, but inevitably I will revert to my self-defeating thoughts and behaviors when a crisis arises in my life.

In order to truly change, I must transform my view of who I am, not just what I do. I must embrace God's reality as my own through the process of reflection. What does that look like? For me, it could include a combination of the following:

- reading Scripture multiple times (often with the help of studies or commentaries to put the context in perspective)
- reading books by godly men and women who speak truth and encouragement into my life
- listening to great preachers and teachers as I walk with my iPod or drive in my car
- sitting alone in silence, asking the Lord to speak to my heart and reinforce his truths to me
- meeting with Christian friends to go deeper into God's Word and to hold each other accountable

I can tell you from experience that these intentional acts of mind renewal—repetition, concentration, and reflection—will lead to complete transformation in your life! And much like training for that marathon, it will not be easy at first. However, the more you devote yourself to this process, the more it will become a natural habit in your life—it will also bring you a sense of absolute joy and peace.

As we close this week of our journey together, I encourage you to take a moment to read and meditate on the following passage several times. Sit quietly before the Lord, and reflect on what this verse means to you at this moment. Use the space below to journal your thoughts.

You grew weary in your search,
    but you never gave up.
Desire gave you renewed strength,
    and you did not grow weary.   Isaiah 57:10

Part III:
Embracing Your Future

Week 5

Introduction

Recommended Reading From *Named by God*: Chapters 14–16
Named by God Video Curriculum: DVD Session 5

[Jesus said,] "If you want to be my disciple, you must hate everyone else by comparison—your father and mother, wife and children, brothers and sisters—yes, even your own life. Otherwise, you cannot be my disciple. And if you do not carry your own cross and follow me, you cannot be my disciple. But don't begin until you count the cost. For who would begin construction of a building without first calculating the cost to see if there is enough money to finish it? Otherwise, you might complete only the foundation before running out of money, and then everyone would laugh at you."

LUKE 14:26-29

This passage may be one of the most controversial and misrepresented passages in all of Scripture. But I believe it is also one of the richest, so let's dive in and see what it has to say to us this week.

First, let's spend a few moments breaking apart these particular words spoken from the mouth of our Lord. They are some of the most challenging yet most beautiful words that Jesus spoke during his time on earth. And they certainly have the power to sober up those of us who have had a little too much of the world's influence!

In this passage Jesus describes what it means to follow him—in other words, to truly call yourself a disciple. He is not asking, "What do you believe?" but "What kind of life do you live in light of what you believe?"

Jesus knew that people of any culture flock to the path of least resistance. In other words, we quit far too easily. All around us, people are quitting on their marriages, quitting on their children, quitting on their friendships, quitting on an education, quitting on a job, quitting on the pursuit of God's plan for their lives.

Jesus speaks directly to this human tendency and says, in effect, "Whatever you do, don't quit—especially when it comes to being my follower!"

You see, anything that matters in this life is going to cost us something. That includes being Jesus' disciple. As Jesus well knew, a life devoted to following him will be full of hardship and challenge, so he takes this opportunity to say, "When the going gets tough, you are going to want to give up. But don't quit! Great sacrifice equals great reward."

The particularly interesting thing about this passage is the use of the word *hate*. And it comes in an unexpected place—in reference to those closest to us. It's a bit of a surprise coming from Jesus, since no one on earth is more loving than he is. And yet here he uses a word that seems to be the opposite of love—hate.

In order to unpack this passage accurately, we must understand the word *hate* in this context as Jesus meant it. Jesus isn't saying here that we should mistreat our families or loved ones; he is saying that we need to "love them less." In other words, being in a relationship with Jesus must be in an altogether different category from any of our other relationships. No one else can be as significant to us as he is. Jesus' strong statement here is not intended to be insensitive but to draw our attention to the fact that nothing else should come close to our pursuit and love of him. That's right—even spouses, parents, and children must come second to our love for and pursuit of Jesus Christ.

In practical terms, this means that you are bound to face relational pressures when you put Jesus first in your life. This could come in the form of your parents, who encourage you not to be so "radical" about your faith. It could come in the form of your spouse, who thinks you are taking this Christianity thing a little too far. The pressure might even be in the form of your children, who get angry with you for not approving of their worldly behaviors.

Every day we must ask ourselves these questions: How important is my relationship with Jesus? Am I willing to carry my cross to follow him today?

Carrying your cross means that you are a dead man (or woman) walking—you are willing to lay down your life right now for the sake of Christ.

But take heart—his glory is your reward.

Group Session 5

Life, like war, is a series of mistakes, and he is not the best Christian nor the best general who makes the fewest false steps . . . but he is the best who wins the most splendid victories by the retrieval of mistakes. Forget mistakes; organize victories out of mistakes.

BRITISH PREACHER F. W. ROBERTSON

A mistake is an opportunity to begin again, this time more intelligently.   HENRY FORD

This week we will be tackling a big topic: does your faith produce life-changing results, the kind we read about in the Bible? We will be challenged to believe that the courageous faith we read about in Scripture is the same faith we have access to today. We will hear the call to be bold about our faith and to live the lives God has created us and saved us for.

1. He knows that we will default to our _____ every time; therefore, he requires _____ .

If we are unfaithful, he remains faithful, for he cannot deny who he is.   2 TIMOTHY 2:13

2. Our faith in God should not come from our ability to _____ God, to _____ God, to _____ God, or to _____ God. Our faith should solely rest on *his* ability to be _____ .

3. When God speaks to you, it is either in encouragement, blessing, or discipline.

You must not interpret your down times as _____ . God never calls a _____ on your life.

"What have you done to us? Why did you make us leave Egypt? Didn't we tell you this would happen while we were still in Egypt? We said, 'Leave us alone! Let us be slaves to the Egyptians. It's better to be a slave in Egypt than a corpse in the wilderness!'" But Moses told the people, "Don't be afraid.

Just stand still and watch the LORD rescue you today. The Egyptians you see today will never be seen again. The LORD himself will fight for you. Just stay calm." Then the LORD said to Moses, "Why are you crying out to me? Tell the people to get moving! Pick up your staff and raise your hand over the sea. Divide the water so the Israelites can walk through the middle of the sea on dry ground."

EXODUS 14:11-16

4. Seizing God's vision for your life means you will not spend one more moment simply

_____ this world, but through obedience and trust,

_____ the day for the glory of God.

5. When God begins to reveal his promise and his purpose for your life, he will always take the

_____ .

Why? Because the _____ is the _____ !

God is more concerned about your character than he is about your comfort!

Day 1

Wear Lightweight Clothing

In your mind, picture a smooth asphalt road stretching into the distance. The tips of your sneakers are poised on a bright-yellow strip that has been painted across the pavement. As your eyes strain toward the horizon, you notice a small flicker catching the sun's rays. You squint harder and strain forward. Yes, something is there—at the very end of the road. Light dances in every direction from the brilliant gold edges. And if you're not mistaken, there are even jewels—diamonds, rubies, sapphires—more jewels than you've ever seen in one place.

The race is about to begin, and the crown is yours if you so desire. Now that you think about it, the finish line doesn't even seem that far away. If you run instead of walk, you could get there faster. But as you take a deep breath and break into a sprint, you notice something else ahead. Right in the middle of the road stands a huge hill. And just in front of that, you spot a gaping hole. But you know what a beautiful prize awaits you in the distance, so you keep running.

It's not long before your view of the finish line is obscured by the hills and obstacles in your path. You lose focus for a moment, and suddenly . . . bam! Ouch! You trip on a pothole in the road and fall flat on your face. *Wow! This road is bumpier than I thought.* You pick yourself up and start running again, but this time you're going to make sure you keep your eyes focused on your goal.

> *Let us strip off every weight that slows us down, especially the sin that so easily trips us up. And let us run with endurance the race God has set before us. We do this by keeping our eyes on Jesus, the champion who initiates and perfects our faith.*   Hebrews 12:1-2

As you begin your study time today, get quiet before Jesus, the "champion who initiates and perfects our faith." Praise him for the path he has set before you—the course he has marked out for you and the prize of abundant living that awaits you. Give him all your gratitude, for this prize is far more than you could ever dream or deserve. Ask him to reveal to you anything that is slowing you down in your race.

We will spend week 5 together in training. By the end of this week, you should be equipped and ready for some long-distance running. The marathon you are training for is no ordinary race—it is your life! And the fitness instructor who is working with you is none other than your Creator.

Our first lesson as we strive toward our fitness goal addresses this question: What do I wear to the race? Sounds easy, right? You've got good fashion sense and a closet full of clothes. That may be true, but this lesson has nothing to do with your eye for style.

1. **Read Hebrews 12:1-3.**

What does verse 1 say you are to do with anything that slows you down or trips you up?

_____

_____

2. **What distractions are keeping you from running at your maximum speed? What articles of clothing need to be thrown off? (This could be certain habits, relationships, hobbies, television shows, etc.) Please list them below.**

_____

_____

_____

_____

_____

_____

Along with evaluating our attire for the race, we also need to pay close attention to a few mile markers along the way to make sure we stay on course.

Mile Marker 1: Surround Yourself with Committed Runners

3. **Match each of the Scriptures below to the corresponding characteristic a friend should demonstrate.**

Proverbs 11:13   always loyal; loves at all times

Proverbs 17:9   willing to say hard things that are in your best interest

Proverbs 17:17   trustworthy; does not gossip

Proverbs 27:6   looks past an offense; forgives faults

4. **List at least three people currently in your life whom you would consider close friends.**

_____

_____

_____

When you look at the names you listed, what characteristics come to mind in regard to each person? Are these friends who love you despite your past, despite any future mistakes you might make? Or are these friends who tend to judge you and condemn your sin as being worse than their own? When you spend time with these friends, are you so busy talking about other people that you don't have time to build each other up in your relationship with Christ? Do these friends go along with you in your moments of self-pity, saying things like, "I can't believe she said that about you—how rude" or "You just need to forget about him. Let's go key his car"? Or do your friends speak Scripture into your life in the midst of rough situations, even when it's difficult for you to hear?

5. **Is there anyone in your life you need to distance yourself from in order to be a more effective follower of Christ? Use the person's initials if you'd like.**

_____

_____

_____

_____

Mile Marker 2: Detox Your System

At some point in your journey of faith, you will realize that, although salvation is free, obedience to the Lord can be quite costly. If you want to live a life that is free of the worries and fears of this world, you will need to sacrifice the distractions that have seeped in and taken priority over your relationship with Jesus.

6. **Place a check by any addiction below (private or public) that you are currently struggling with.**

_____ I read unwholesome books or magazines.

_____ I watch television programs or movies that are not God honoring.

_____ I visit inappropriate websites.

_____ I view and forward distasteful e-mails to my friends or coworkers.

_____ I use distasteful language or crude humor in my communication with others.

_____ I talk about other people behind their backs.

_____ I habitually use a tobacco product.

_____ I am addicted to alcohol.

_____ I abuse over-the-counter medications.

_____ I often turn to food for comfort or to numb negative feelings.

_____ I spend numerous hours of my day focusing on my body and appearance (working out, tanning, shopping, applying makeup).

_____ I spend numerous hours of my day on the Internet (e-mail, Facebook, Twitter, etc.).

_____ I am consumed with being successful at my job.

_____ I am consumed with making my home and children as perfect as possible.

_____ I am in a habit of missing church regularly.

_____ I allow days or even weeks to pass without picking up my Bible.

_____ I am addicted to sleeping or being lazy.

_____ I can't think about a certain person without feeling bitter or jealous.

_____ I am a people pleaser—I live in fear of other people's opinions of me.

Since you have heard about Jesus and have learned the truth that comes from him, throw off your old sinful nature and your former way of life, which is corrupted by lust and deception. Instead, let the Spirit renew your thoughts and attitudes. Put on your new nature, created to be like God— truly righteous and holy.　　　　　　　　　　　　　　　　　　　　EPHESIANS 4:21-24

God has a big plan for you that is beyond your imagination. But in order to make room for it, you will first need to cut out the small, selfish places that threaten to obscure it. The longer you wait to sacrifice those unhealthy addictions, the longer you postpone the true desires of your heart.

As you end your time with the Lord today, offer the following prayer to him:

Lord, help me to own up to the selfishness and strongholds I am hanging on to. Give me the strength to pursue your immeasurably better plans for my life over my selfish desires. I want to cut out the following people and addictions from my life in order to become more like your Son, Jesus.

(Feel free to journal your prayer below.)

_____

_____

_____

_____

_____

_____

_____

_____

_____

_____

_____

_____

_____

_____

_____

Day 2

Help Others When They Fall

Take a moment to offer up a prayer before the Lord, asking him to use today's study time to reveal how you can be more servant minded. Ask him to show you the people and places that need you to be on their teams today. Ask him to open your heart to areas of laziness or procrastination that hold you back from service.

Let's begin our day with a good dose of truth!

Read the following passages, and fill in the blanks.

1. **Read Galatians 6:2.**

   Share, or carry, each other's _____ .

2. **Read Ephesians 4:12.**

   Equip God's people to do his work and _____ the church, the body of Christ.

3. **Read 1 John 4:21.**

   Those who love God must also love their Christian _____ and

   _____ .

4. **Read 1 Peter 4:11.**

   Everything you do will bring _____ to God through Jesus Christ.

5. **Read the beautiful story about Jesus in John 13:1-17.**

   Write verse 15 below.

   _____

   _____

_____

_____

_____

_____

_____

_____

_____

_____

_____

As Jesus and his disciples gather for the Passover feast, it is obvious to all those in attendance that someone needs to wash their feet. But there is a pause—no one immediately volunteers. That's likely because in the culture of Jesus' time, that responsibility was reserved for those seen as the lowliest of the group. None of the disciples is jumping at the opportunity to be the "least."

And then, amid hushed gulps of air and subtle whispers, Jesus takes a towel and washbasin, wraps the towel around his waist, and proceeds to wash the caked-on dirt from each of his friends' feet.

In doing so, Jesus showed what greatness truly is—having the heart and mind of a servant.

6. **When you attend church, which comment do you find yourself saying more often?**

_____ "What is this church going to do to meet my needs?"

_____ "What can I do to meet the needs of this church?"

7. **List some ways in which you currently serve your local body of believers.**

_____

_____

_____

_____

_____

8. **If you are having a difficult time thinking of things you do to serve the body of believers, what may be holding you back from accepting God's call to serve?**

_____

_____

_____

_____

_____

Serving is a difficult call to follow. I can honestly say that I would rather hear Jesus ask me to leave everything in order to follow him than make myself nothing to serve other people. Many of us (myself included) love the rush of adventure that comes with giving up everything or moving to a new place in the name of the Lord. However, I don't jump at the opportunity to hand over my clothes to my enemy or walk an extra mile with someone who is completely undeserving. Yet this is the defining mark of a true follower of Christ—a selfless servant.

In the area of service, there is no spotlight, no fame, no grandiose adventure. True service to the Lord is not self-righteous. It does not seek human recognition or reward. True service is not picky about whom to serve or when it would be most convenient. True service does not stem from "feeling" like serving but from being called to serve.

9. In light of this description, what are some things that need to change in your attitude or perspective or actions in order to truly serve God?

_____

_____

_____

_____

_____

_____

_____

_____

God has given each of you a gift from his great variety of spiritual gifts. Use them well to serve one another. Do you have the gift of speaking? Then speak as though God himself were speaking through you. Do you have the gift of helping others? Do it with all the strength and energy that God supplies. Then everything you do will bring glory to God through Jesus Christ. All glory and power to him forever and ever! Amen.
1 PETER 4:10-11

As we end our time together today, spend a few moments with the Lord. As you pray, close your eyes and picture Jesus kneeling before you with a towel wrapped around his waist, gently wiping the dirt from your feet. Ask God to let his kind of service resonate ever so powerfully within the recesses of your heart. Pray for new eyes to see everyone around you—your church, your family, complete strangers, and even your enemies—as those you might serve in Jesus' name.

Day 3

The Gold Medalist inside You

Before we get started, let's commit our time to God. I pray that the past few weeks of prayer and study have begun to help you develop a habit of meeting with the Lord on a daily basis. I hope you have enjoyed getting quiet before him and opening your heart to him, as well as hearing his voice speak to you. I hope you have learned to treasure the Scriptures—the very breath of the Almighty.

Today, praise God for the gifts he has so lovingly lavished on you. Pray that he will grant you the wisdom to pinpoint your abilities and the strength to see yourself as worthy to use them for his glory.

1. **Let's begin by doing a little self-evaluation. Make a list of the gifts you believe you possess. This is not the time to be shy—be confident in the Lord! Make your list as exhaustive as possible. Even if there are gifts you haven't used for a while or gifts that have never been put into action, include them on the list. Think of as many traits as you can that might benefit the Lord and others.**

_____

_____

_____

_____

_____

_____

_____

_____

2. **How can you use those gifts to serve others in the body of Christ?**

_____

_____

_____

_____

_____

_____

_____

3. **Read 1 Corinthians 12:1-11.**

Verse 4 states that although there are different gifts, there is the same _____ .

Verse 6 states that although God works in different ways, the same _____

_____ works in us all.

4. **Read Ephesians 4:7.**

Christians have been given gifts, and grace, because of whose generosity?

_____

_____

5. **Read 1 Peter 4:10 and 1 Corinthians 12:7.**

According to these verses, what is the purpose of our spiritual gifts?

_____

_____

6. **Read 1 Corinthians 12:12-31.**

Fill in the blanks from this passage of Scripture.

If one part suffers, what happens to the other parts (verse 26)?

_____

_____

If one part is honored, what happens to the other parts (verse 26)?

_____

_____

Reread verse 27. All of us together are Christ's body, and each of us is _____ .

Reread the first part of verse 31 to find out what our attitudes should be toward our spiritual gifts.

Write verse 31 below.

_____

_____

_____

_____

7. Go back to 1 Corinthians 12:1-11 and list the spiritual gifts mentioned in these verses.

_____

_____

_____

_____

_____

_____

_____

8. Read 1 Corinthians 12:27-28. List the spiritual gifts in this passage (some will be duplicates from your previous list).

_____

_____

_____

_____

_____

_____

_____

_____

9. Read Ephesians 4:11. List the spiritual gifts given in this verse (again, you will have duplicates).

_____

_____

_____

_____

_____

_____

_____

10. Read Romans 12:6-8. List the spiritual gifts in this passage of Scripture.

_____

_____

_____

_____

_____

_____

_____

_____

As we wrap up today, I want to remind you that your gift has been given to you not so you can sit on it but so that you might regift it to the world. Then people will be able to see what Jesus looks like through you!

Stay with me on this, blessed child of God, because in day 4, you will have the opportunity to get personal and specific when it comes to these gifts. It's time to unwrap that gift you've left lying around!

Day 4

Don't Forget to Breathe

I pray that today you will gain insight into who you are—your character, your personality, your abilities, your gifts. Take a moment now to ask God to show you the gifts you've been given by the Holy Spirit and to give you the courage to use those gifts for his glory.

In day 3, we devoted much of our time to researching the spiritual gifts set out for us in Scripture. These lists are not meant to be exhaustive—in other words, you may have gifts that don't show up on these lists but are nonetheless intended by God to be used to serve him and others.

A word of warning before we get into your unique gift, however. Oswald Chambers said, "Unguarded strength is actually a double weakness." In other words, if we use the gifts God gave us in the wrong way, they can end up working against God instead of for him.

Another note of caution: whenever we talk about gifts, we need to remember where they come from in the first place. God doesn't bestow certain gifts and abilities on us because we are good or deserving. In fact, according to Scripture, God is in the business of choosing people first and then filling them with a particular gifting and anointing.

God anoints ordinary people to do extraordinary things, as he did in the case of Moses.

The LORD said to Moses, "Look, I have specifically chosen Bezalel son of Uri, grandson of Hur, of the tribe of Judah. I have filled him with the Spirit of God, giving him great wisdom, ability, and expertise in all kinds of crafts. He is a master craftsman, expert in working with gold, silver, and bronze. He is skilled in engraving and mounting gemstones and in carving wood. He is a master at every craft!"
EXODUS 31:1-5

Go back to the passage, and circle the words that indicate Bezalel's gift ultimately came from God.

It's interesting to note that this is the first time in Scripture that we see this particular word usage—that God "filled" a human with his Spirit. It's also fascinating that God isn't choosing this man to be a preacher, an author, a speaker, a singer, or a businessman. No, God chooses this man to be an artist, a carpenter.

1. **Read Psalm 103:5.**

   God fills our lives and satisfies our desires with what?

   _____

   _____

   _____

2. **What is something you truly desire to do for the benefit of others? Journal your answer below. (Note that there are no big or small answers to this question. You could be passionate about anything from visiting the elderly in a nursing home to starting a women's Bible study to tutoring someone from another country to becoming a preacher. There is no limit to your desires. List as many as you can think of.)**

   _____

   _____

   _____

   _____

   _____

   _____

   _____

   _____

   _____

3. **Look back at the list above, and write down all the activities you currently _aren't_ pursuing.**

   _____

   _____

   _____

   _____

   _____

   _____

   _____

   _____

   _____

4. **What are some things you're good at? Journal your answer below. (This could include things such as baking, encouraging, organizing, listening, praying, etc. Think of things that come naturally to you and also bring you joy.)**

   _____

   _____

_____

_____

_____

_____

_____

_____

_____

_____

5. What areas of opportunity are currently available in your church and/or community? Journal your response below. (List every area you are aware of, regardless of whether you feel you are capable of handling such responsibilities.)

_____

_____

_____

_____

_____

_____

_____

_____

_____

_____

6. I pray that the Lord has granted you some insight into the gifts he has placed inside you.

Take a moment to write out a prayer of gratitude to the Lord for the gifts and abilities he has bestowed on you. Also write a precise commitment to serve in a specific area of your church or community. Be specific about what you will do, how you will begin, and when you will start.

_____

_____

_____

_____

_____

_____

_____

_____

Day 5

The Beauty of the Race

Today will be our final day of strength training. We will conclude with an awesome reminder of why we entered this race in the first place—the prize!

Please take a moment to praise God for the insights he has given you throughout your study this week. Ask God to refresh your spirit as you continue in this journey we call life.

When we keep our eyes fixed on the prize of Jesus Christ, the race we are running almost instantly seems full of clarity and purpose.

1. Read John 12:23-28, and answer the following questions.

What is the fate of someone who loves his or her life?

_____

_____

What is the reward for someone who cares nothing for (or hates, NIV) his or her life?

_____

_____

In the context of this passage, what do you think it means to care nothing for, or hate, your life?

_____

_____

_____

_____

_____

_____

_____

_____

2. Read Luke 22:41-49. Although Jesus' heart is troubled, is he spared from completing his mission?

_____

_____

3. Read John 12:44-50.

In verse 47, Jesus says his mission is not to judge the world but to _____ !

Who does Jesus say has given him the words to say and how to say them (verse 49)?

_____

_____

4. Read John 19:28-30.

Write the final words of Jesus. _____ .

Jesus is the only one who will ever perfectly complete the race God set out for him to run. But God still calls us to run faithfully, with the help he provides. No matter what your spiritual gift is, no matter what your background or personality type or family history, the one thing God calls you to do is to share about his prize with other people.

5. Read 2 Timothy 4:5. How many times have you taken the opportunity to tell another person about the beautiful story of Christ's work in your life? (Circle one.)

never

once or twice

I've tried a few times.

on a weekly basis

almost every day

6. If you've never shared the Good News of Jesus Christ with another person, what fears or worries have kept you from doing so?

_____

_____

_____

_____

_____

There are way more things in our lives that we *can* do than things we *should* do. If Satan can't prevent us from being Christians, he will keep us so busy doing "Christian things" that we completely miss our calling in Christ. If Satan can't get us to do bad things, he will keep us so distracted with *good* things that we will inevitably do the bad things after all. We can't afford to get off the course of the race God has set before us, no matter how innocent the side path may seem.

We must not get so distracted with our potential that we completely miss our calling.

Here is the visual image that helps me when I think about our main purpose in life: The calling to bring lost people to the cross of Christ is the title of your book. It is the one overarching theme that covers you completely and oversees everything you do. The subtitle of your book, however, can vary. It may read mother, daughter, wife, friend, sister, aunt, employee, leader, and so on. You must not confuse the title of your book with your subtitle.

Next week we will conclude our study by making a commitment to God and to ourselves to carry out our life message: to believe that we have truly been named by God and to begin to live in a way that reflects the very nature of Jesus Christ.

7. **As we close this week's time of study, journal below about one event when God worked powerfully in your life. When you are finished, write down the name of one person you feel God may be wanting you to share part of your life message with.**

_____

_____

_____

_____

_____

_____

_____

_____

_____

_____

_____

_____

Close in prayer, asking the Lord to overwhelm you with the thrill of what thrills him—running the race well and encouraging others to chase the prize alongside you.

Week 6

Introduction

Recommended Reading from *Named by God*: Chapters 17–18, Conclusion
Named by God Video Curriculum: DVD Session 6

As we embark on our final week together, I'd like to look at an interesting passage from the book of Isaiah. In the opening verses of Isaiah 49, we find the prophet Isaiah boldly declaring the calling and purpose the Lord has given him. And then in the sentences immediately following, he is doubting himself completely as a messenger. The passage reads as follows:

> *Listen to me, all you in distant lands!*
> *Pay attention, you who are far away!*
> *The LORD called me before my birth;*
> *from within the womb he called me by name.*
> *He made my words of judgment as sharp as a sword.*
> *He has hidden me in the shadow of his hand.*
> *I am like a sharp arrow in his quiver.*
>
> *He said to me, "You are my servant, Israel,*
> *and you will bring me glory."*
> *I replied, "But my work seems so useless!*
> *I have spent my strength for nothing and to no purpose.*
> *Yet I leave it all in the LORD's hand; I will trust God for my reward."*
>
> *And now the LORD speaks—*
> *the one who formed me in my mother's womb to be his servant,*
> *who commissioned me to bring Israel back to him.*
> *The LORD has honored me,*
> *and my God has given me strength.*   ISAIAH 49:1-5

Let me give you a bit of background here. The Jewish nation has been called to glorify God and to be his light to the Gentile nations. But they are failing the Lord miserably. Therefore, the Lord appoints Isaiah to basically go in and clean up the mess the Israelites left behind. God fills Isaiah with the Holy Spirit and sends him out as a messenger of his love and hope to the nations.

We see Isaiah claim the Lord's anointing on his life with great confidence at first. This is a mission he receives from the very beginning—from within his mother's womb. It is obvious he is aware of God's plan and purpose for him, and he points out that the Lord called him by name before he was even born! He knows the Lord desires him to be a powerful voice to bring his people back to the Lord and to bring the Lord glory.

But then Isaiah turns from full-throttle hero out to save the day to a guy throwing the ultimate pity party!

Does Isaiah's story resonate with anyone besides me? One moment I'm sensing the Lord's direction so clearly, and the next I'm doubting that I heard him speak at all.

You don't need me to tell you how easy it is to lose sight of our high calling in Christ. We get so easily distracted by what is urgent that we don't pay attention to what is important.

The way I see it, there are two major telltale signs when we are starting to lose our vision of God's plan for our lives: worry and discouragement. You see, God's plans and desires for us are so big and brilliant that if he actually allowed us to see the landscape view, it would absolutely boggle our minds. Therefore, he gives us bits and pieces that we can swallow in small doses. The problem is, we can hardly grasp even the bits and pieces. That's when our fears start to creep in and we begin doubting God. In our worry and discouragement, we choose the wasteland of a narrow vision for our lives over the risky road God has called us to. There is only one way to live a rewarding, joyful, purpose-filled existence, and that's to invest in what truly matters. And let me tell you, nothing that gathers dust or will one day burn up falls into that category. The Bible tells us there are only three things that are eternal and worth our investment:

1) **God's Word.** The Bible is the one book that is eternal. God's Word is alive and applicable at any point in history to anyone in history.

   Hold firmly to the word of life. PHILIPPIANS 2:16

   Simon Peter replied, "Lord, to whom would we go? You have the words that give eternal life." JOHN 6:68

   [Jesus said,] "I tell you the truth, anyone who obeys my teaching will never die!" JOHN 8:51

2) **The church.** God created an entire universe simply because he desired a family to love and to be loved by. The body of Christ will last forever.

   The church is his body; it is made full and complete by Christ, who fills all things everywhere with himself. EPHESIANS 1:23

   All of you together are Christ's body, and each of you is a part of it. 1 CORINTHIANS 12:27

   Christ is also the head of the church, which is his body. He is the beginning, supreme over all who rise from the dead. So he is first in everything. COLOSSIANS 1:18

3) **Love.** The only reason you and I are capable of loving another human being is because we were created in the image of the one whose very nature is love. God's love—and the love we give in return—is everlasting.

   Give thanks to the LORD, for he is good!
   His faithful love endures forever. PSALM 136:1

If we desperately desire our lives' counting for something—if we long to catch God's most grandiose vision for us during our time on earth—it's time to get radical. Let's see what God can do with a bunch of wrecks like us!

Welcome to week 6!

Group Session 6

This week we will learn what it looks like to be change makers in our individual spheres of influence. We will discover together that living as ambassadors for Christ is the only way we will be truly happy and complete.

God dares us to go on this adventure with him, just as he's dared his followers for generations. Let's take this opportunity to check in with a group of guys who find themselves smack-dab in the middle of a "Come on, I dare ya" moment.

Read Luke 5:1-11.

1. God doesn't _____ your boat, but he chooses to get into it because *you* are there!

2. God will never go around a _____ instrument.

   God will always use our availability to display his greatness.

3. If we want to be image bearers, we must get out of _____ water and put our nets down _____ .

4. Deep water will always involve a _____ or a _____ of some kind.

5. Deep water will always involve the _____ .

6. Deep water will challenge the way you see _____ and the way you see _____ .

7. Deep water will always involve _____ and have _____ .

8. Deep water will force you to lay down your _____ .

9. Deep water will always grant a _____ .

"Master," Simon replied, "we worked hard all last night and didn't catch a thing. But if you say so, I'll let the nets down again."
                                                                          LUKE 5:5

10. We will save ourselves much suffering in this life if we will make a practice of repeating the phrase

_____

_____

Day 1

Daily Renewal

Let's begin our study time with a sincere prayer before our God. If you aren't sure where to start, use this passage as a prompt for prayer:

That is why we never give up. Though our bodies are dying, our spirits are being renewed every day. For our present troubles are small and won't last very long. Yet they produce for us a glory that vastly outweighs them and will last forever! So we don't look at the troubles we can see now; rather, we fix our gaze on things that cannot be seen. For the things we see now will soon be gone, but the things we cannot see will last forever.   2 CORINTHIANS 4:16-18

Precious Redeemer, I will never give up! For I know that, although this body is dying with each passing day, my spirit is refreshed and renewed each time I step into your presence. Although my current issues and troubles seem all-consuming and overwhelming right now, I pray that you will remind me of the sacrifice and suffering your Son went through on the cross. Please open my eyes to the pain he endured so my current trials might fade to light and momentary bumps in the road. Lord, I pray that for the rest of my days I will see each difficult moment as bringing me closer to the prize— eternal glory with Jesus. Help me to keep my eyes fixed on the eternal, not the temporary. Give me the strength to live each day as though it were my last—as a passionate, bold believer. With all my heart, I serve you and praise your holy name. In the name of your Son, who died for me, amen.

1. **Read the following verses. Next to each, document what is being renewed or being changed in the Scripture passage.**

Psalm 51:10   _____

Psalm 103:5   _____

Isaiah 40:31   _____

Romans 12:2   _____

2. Read Titus 3:4-5. According to this passage, who is responsible for our renewal?

_____

_____

I have to confess to you that for many years I thought *I* was pursuing God. My life radically changed in the moment I realized I wasn't the one doing the pursuing; it was the Lord, in his grace, who was drawing me to himself.

This truth is revelatory to someone who has been brought up within the suffocating walls of tradition, ritual, and religion. I shudder to think that for so long I believed my church attendance, Bible reading, and acts of service somehow made me more worthy of God's love.

For those of you who at this moment may be receiving a bit of a spiritual slap in the face, I implore you not to turn away. Embrace it and ask for another, because this truth will set captives free!

The truth is, you and I are just plain wretched. Left to our own devices, we will always—and I do mean *always*—default to our flesh. We choose self over God every time. Don't kid yourself—this applies to everyone, including Bible study teachers, pastors, worship leaders, and fifty-year Christian veterans. Our inborn natures make us incapable of pursuing and following after God on our own. We don't choose him; in his grace and mercy, he chooses us! Wow.

It is only through the Holy Spirit's movement in us that we are able to respond to the Lord's pursuit of us.

This is precisely why Satan is capable of showing up at church and sitting right next to you in your favorite pew. In fact, Satan doesn't really have a problem with your attending church, going to small group, reading your Bible, singing in the choir, or serving in ministry . . . as long as you're doing it for the wrong reasons. Maybe you do it because people expect it or because you feel compelled to check something off your spiritual to-do list or because you're trying to impress others or because it makes you feel good about yourself. Jesus gives a sobering warning about doing the right things for the wrong reasons: "On judgment day many will say to me, 'Lord! Lord! We prophesied in your name and cast out demons in your name and performed many miracles in your name.' But I will reply, 'I never knew you. Get away from me, you who break God's laws'" (Matthew 7:22-23).

There is only one way to make sure our service is pleasing to God, and that is to make sure we remain on the Holy Spirit's life support. The Holy Spirit is the channel through whom God speaks to and pursues his children. But it is not enough to simply have head knowledge of how and why the Holy Spirit works. We must experience him firsthand and invite him to take over our lives on a daily basis.

Being filled with the Holy Spirit is a little like putting gas in your car. It's not something you do just once—and you can't go very far without stopping to refill. Trust me, you know when your tank is on empty. There is tension in your marriage, you are struggling with your spending, you're facing dissension with your coworkers and your friends, you are anxious all the time, you are not sleeping well, and it seems as if all your joy is gradually being sucked dry. If that sounds like you, you just might be in need of a fill-up!

3. In John 14:26 Jesus states that who will give you the Holy Spirit?

_____

_____

4. In John 14:26 Jesus goes on to say that the Spirit will _____ you everything and _____ you of everything Jesus has said.

5. Read Galatians 5:19-23.

List the "fruit of the Spirit" described in this passage (there are nine).

_____

_____

_____

_____

_____

_____

_____

_____

_____

Now list the "filth of the flesh" mentioned in these verses (there are fifteen).

_____

_____

_____

_____

_____

_____

_____

_____

_____

_____

_____

_____

_____

_____

_____

The Holy Spirit has the power to bring the only kind of lasting transformation. Let the Spirit renew and refresh you today and each day that follows, from here until eternity. Take the heavy burden of legalism off your shoulders, and bask in God's pursuit of you.

If you're ready to be changed by the Holy Spirit, it's time to make a covenant between you and God. Commit to calling on God each morning, asking him to fill you with the power of his Holy Spirit. If you are willing to make this commitment, place your initials in the space below.

_____

Day 2

The Path of the Wise

When a pastor or Bible study teacher introduces a new series or lesson on the topic of wisdom, many of us roll our eyes, cross our arms, and let out a sigh of anticipated boredom. We think, *Come on. Wisdom? Let's talk about something more interesting, like the end times or maybe sex.*

Pardon me for being bold here (because I am definitely speaking to myself as well), but I think the real reason we shirk the topic is because the more we understand the importance of biblical wisdom, the more we understand how lacking in wisdom we truly are!

As we go through this final week of our study together, my desire is to challenge all of us to our very core! I want to dare you to live radically for Christ. In order to present a challenge that is worthy of God's Word, I must pull out the big guns. You might be as surprised as I was to hear that wisdom is one of the big guns. But it wasn't until I started a quest for wisdom that I realized how unwise I really was.

Wisdom is the glue that holds our lives together. But I am convinced that this is an area where Christians tend to flat out miss the mark. The book of Proverbs is chock-full of ways people tend to live unwisely. When we are complacent, we are foolish (see 1:32). When we talk too much and ramble on, we are foolish (see 10:8). When we believe our way is the only way, we are foolish (see 12:15). When we befriend and hang out with the wrong people, we are foolish (see 13:20). When we argue and quarrel with others, we are foolish (see 20:3).

Wisdom is the hinge between . . .

- what you do and do not know about Christ.
- what you do and do not know about God's Word.
- what you do and do not know about others.
- what you do and do not know about yourself.

If so many important factors of life hinge on wisdom, why do so many of us place this biblical truth on the back burner?

I personally believe it is because humans tend to *under*value wisdom. Instead of looking at wisdom as something to be continually growing in and searching for, these people wrongly believe (with pride at the root) that their lives can be sustained on their current level of understanding. These people most likely became overwhelmed, stressed out, discouraged, or distracted at some point in their lives, and as a result, grew content to rest on what they know and who they know; this level of wisdom certainly allows them the luxury of paying the bills and hanging out with the "gang" on Friday night, but at the core of their lives, a deep sense of value is missing. They have not only stopped searching for wisdom, but they have also given up on a more rewarding, purpose-filled life and, at the same time, are forfeiting a future of abundant, God-shaped possibilities.

One more interesting thing to note about wisdom is that it requires a continual search. We never "arrive" at the point of being all-wise. Wisdom is a process, an everyday pursuit.

Wisdom is not something to be treated lightly or sought halfheartedly. It should be pursued with the intensity of someone who has found the love of her life and will do anything to make sure he doesn't get away.

When my husband and I were dating, he was all I thought about. He was the only person I wanted to be with. As if he were my homework, I *studied* him. I invested time and energy learning his background, his likes and dislikes, his silly quirks that made him who he was. That's the kind of passion we need as we chase after wisdom.

As we continue in today's study of the Word, take a moment now to ask God for supernatural wisdom. Boldly pray for wisdom that is far beyond your years and your experience. Ask him to make you smarter than you really are!

Wisdom can be defined as "the ability to recognize right from wrong" or "the ability to make good use of knowledge." It's not just about being smart; it's about putting head knowledge into action.

I believe that God can give us the ability to discern between right and wrong. And when we get a little fuzzy on that count, the Holy Spirit (our great Counselor) can set us straight.

How about you? Do you make good use of the knowledge you've been given? Let's take a pop quiz to find out.

1. In the blanks below, place a number (1–7) that most accurately fits each statement.

_____ On average, how many times per week do you ask God to make you wise in a specific area of your life?

_____ On average, how many times per week do you sit in silence with the Lord and allow his voice to speak wisdom to your heart?

_____ On average, how many times per week do you open your Bible and glean wisdom from its pages?

_____ On average, how many times per week do you seek advice or encouragement from godly mentors, wise friends, or counselors?

_____ On average, how many times per week do you read articles, books, or online resources written by Christian authors to help you grow in your faith?

Add all the numbers together to get your total score.

If your total is in the **0–5** range, there's no doubt about it—your life is desperate for more wisdom! But don't be discouraged—choose one area to focus on first, and commit to growing in that area today.

If your total is in the **5–18** range, you are on your way to pursuing godly wisdom, but you could still make better use of the wisdom available to you. Your relationship with Christ and others will definitely benefit from your kicking it up a notch!

If your total is anything **above 18**, congratulations! You are most likely making the pursuit of wisdom a priority in your life. Chasing after godly wisdom has most likely become a habit for you. Keep it up. But remember, there is always room to grow in wisdom; you will never "arrive."

2. **Were you surprised by any of your quiz results? If you found yourself disappointed as you reflected on the role wisdom has in your life, what is one step you can take today to make gaining wisdom more of a priority?**

_____

_____

_____

_____

_____

_____

_____

_____

_____

_____

In our quest for wisdom, what better place to start than the man God named the wisest man who ever lived?

Read 1 Kings 4:29-34.

Allow me to introduce you to King Solomon, the third king of Israel. He is King David's son and chosen heir. As we look at Scripture, we see that, although he does not always lead an exemplary moral life, his daily pursuit of wisdom is something to admire.

Let's take a look at David's promise to make Solomon king, as well as David's final words to his son before handing over the kingdom.

Read 1 Kings 1:28-35; 2:1-4.

3. **Early in Solomon's reign, he establishes himself as one who treasures wisdom. Let's take a peek into the first official meeting between Solomon and his "commanding officer." Read 1 Kings 3:5-15.**

Fill in the blanks from verse 9.

Solomon asks God to give him a(n) _____ to govern his

people well and to know the difference between _____

and _____ .

In verse 5, God gives Solomon the opportunity to ask for anything! He could have asked for wealth, success, a bigger kingdom, a beautiful wife, or for the people to love and adore him.

4. **If God appeared to you right now and gave you the opportunity to ask him for anything, what would you ask for? (Be honest!)**

_____
_____
_____
_____
_____
_____
_____
_____
_____

Solomon chooses wisely—he asks for more wisdom. What does Scripture tell us will happen when we ask for wisdom?

5. **Read James 1:5.**

Under what conditions does God grant us wisdom?

_____
_____
_____

As we see in the communication between Solomon and God, wisdom always begins with the Lord. It is a gift from your heavenly Father that is given in abundance and completely free of charge. The only requirement is that you must go in search of it. Wisdom is given to those who earnestly seek it, not to those who halfheartedly read their Bibles when it's convenient.

I encourage you to take the time to read Proverbs 2–4 to receive a broader understanding of the biblical view of wisdom. Through these chapters, you will gain practical insights into how to pursue wisdom on a daily basis. Here are a few things about wisdom we can glean from these chapters in Proverbs:

- God invites you to ask him for wisdom (2:3).
- Search for wisdom as if searching for treasure (2:4).
- Follow the example of good, righteous people (2:20).
- Do not forget the teachings given to you in God's Word (3:1).
- Trust the Lord in everything, and put no confidence in what you *think* you know (3:5).
- Fear the Lord, and run from all evil (3:7).
- Honor God with your money (3:9).
- When the Lord disciplines you, accept it gratefully (3:11).
- Do not worry about bad things happening to you. Instead, be confident in the Lord (3:25-26).
- When it is in your power to help someone in need, do not hesitate to do so (3:27-28).

- Do not intentionally hurt someone else (3:29).
- Do not turn away from godly teaching (4:2).
- Whatever you do to acquire wisdom will be worth it (4:7).

> *Listen carefully to my words.*
> *Don't lose sight of them.*
> *Let them penetrate deep into your heart,*
> *for they bring life to those who find them,*
> *and healing to their whole body.* PROVERBS 4:20-22

Are you willing to begin a passionate pursuit of wisdom? Write your initials in the space below if you are willing to commit to making God's Word a daily part of your life. Only write your initials if you are willing to open your Bible every day and read at least one chapter.

_____

Day 3

Authentic Light

If we are going to live in passionate pursuit of the Savior, it is vital that we learn to embrace authenticity. To be authentic means that we are genuine and honest about who we have been, who we are, and who we desire to be.

Today I strive to be an open book about my past, present, and future, but it hasn't always been that way. Throughout most of my teenage years, I had a reputation for having it all together. In high school I was very active in my local church and involved in all kinds of "good girl" activities. By the time I was a junior, I had made a name for myself as the outgoing Christian girl. I was even nominated as the president of the high school prayer team. I would proudly wear my "Jesus Rocks" T-shirt and weigh down my right arm with "What Would Jesus Do?" bracelets (yes, that craze took place in my era). I assure you that I looked the part. But inside was another story.

Please know that this wasn't an issue of my salvation—I was most certainly a born-again child of God. I had committed my life to Christ in my pastor's office at the age of nine. I remember, down to the smallest detail, that precious moment in my life. I remember what my pastor said. I remember what I said. I remember the smell of freshly brewed coffee emanating from the nearby kitchen. I remember that my pastor was chomping on a peppermint as he asked, "Kasey, do you understand who Jesus is and what it means to accept him as your personal Savior?"

I remember how I felt leaving the church that day. There were no bells or flashing lights. An angel did not appear to me with a heavenly chorus and sing, "You're saved, you're saved— hallelujah!" I simply remember the peace that consumed me, the peace that went beyond my youthful understanding. But most of all, I remember the conviction. From that moment on, when I did something wrong, it haunted me for days. When I talked back to my mom or lied to my little brother, it bothered me.

There was no doubt about it, I was saved. But to put it plainly, I talked the talk, but I didn't walk the walk. I gave everyone around me the impression that I was completely devoted to Christ. Did I mention that one of the school activities I was involved in was the drama team? And if I do say so myself, I was quite a good actress!

Jesus had some strong words to say about the Pharisees, who were the ultimate example of those who look good on the outside but are living by another set of standards. In Jesus' time, to be a religious leader was to live a life of fame. The Pharisees were well known and respected, and they were among the most powerful members of the community. But as is often the case—back then and today—their status made them hungry for more recognition. They began to lose sight of God and the heart of his teachings.

Practice and obey whatever they tell you, but don't follow their example. For they don't practice what they teach. They crush people with unbearable religious demands and never lift a finger to ease the burden. MATTHEW 23:3-4

Quiet yourself before the Lord in prayer right now. Ask him to reveal any area in your life in which you are saying one thing but doing another. Ask him to shed his light on the dark areas of insincerity, deceit, or artificial living that may have a current foothold in your life. I realize this is a tough topic, and I'm probably going to step on some toes here. But, child of God, if you are serious about living a more daring and sold-out life for Christ, you must be willing to get a little sore in the process. Without challenges, without discipline, without refinement, we will never move beyond an average faith, an ordinary life. Cry out to the Lord, and ask him to break your heart where necessary. Ask him for the strength to walk the walk while talking the talk.

1. **Read Matthew 23:13-36.**

   In your Bible, circle each time Jesus uses the word *hypocrite*.

   hypocrite = a person who puts on a false appearance of virtue; a pretender

   How many instances of the word do you find in this passage?

   _____

   _____

   In order to be authentic believers, we need to make sure our speech matches our actions and our actions match our hearts.

   I'm going to be bold again, so watch your toes. The reason many individuals believe our churches are full of hypocrites is because they are!

2. **Read Matthew 23:5-7.**

   According to verse 5, everything the Pharisees did was for what purpose?

   _____

   _____

Man-made laws and traditions are not always a bad thing. Some of these traditions originated in the early churches described in Scripture and are an important part of our Christian history. These traditions can be beautiful parts of worship if approached with the right heart. But they cross the line when people start taking them more seriously than God-made laws—or when they are done to make us look good rather than to bring glory to God. Using God's law and resources for any reason other than to make God famous is simply a form of hypocrisy.

3. **What does Jesus call the Pharisees in Matthew 23:33?**

_____

_____

4. **Matthew 23:25 compares the religious teachers to dishes. The outside is clean, but the inside is full of what?**

_____

_____

5. **Read Matthew 7:1-5.**

According to this passage, what must we first do before we can see clearly?

_____

_____

In other words, we need to get real with ourselves and our stuff! We all have stuff we need to deal with in our lives. The problem is, we don't like to own up to it. It's smelly and nasty and embarrassing. But if we desire to live authentically and reach people for Christ, we cannot approach them with an "I'm better than you" attitude. They will swiftly see through such a charade and retreat in the opposite direction.

Let me be clear, I'm not encouraging you to air your dirty laundry to everyone you meet. Like I said before, the past is in the past—let's keep it there. Please, for your own sake and everyone else's, keep your mess in the trash heap where it belongs. The point is not that you should ramble on about every sin you've ever struggled with and every pit you've ever jumped into. The point is to simply be real about your sin, no matter how big or small it is in the world's eyes.

In God's view, there are no levels of sin. We are all on the same team, and we are all a bunch of messed-up sinners in need of a Redeemer. Now let's start acting like it! Especially in front of our fellow brothers and sisters in Christ.

I, a prisoner for serving the Lord, beg you to lead a life worthy of your calling, for you have been called by God. Always be humble and gentle. Be patient with each other, making allowance for each other's faults because of your love. Make every effort to keep yourselves united in the Spirit, binding yourselves together with peace. For there is one body and one Spirit, just as you have been called to one glorious hope for the future. There is one Lord, one faith, one baptism, and one God and Father, who is over all and in all and living through all. Ephesians 4:1-6

6. **Take a few moments and journal your thoughts below. List any areas in which you may not be living authentically. Is it the way you talk, an activity you take part in, the way you dress, an attitude of criticism in your heart? Be honest before the Lord as you list any instances of artificial living on your part.**

_____

_____

_____

_____

_____

_____

_____

_____

_____

_____

7. **What are some changes you can make today that will help you to walk the walk as well as talk the talk?**

_____

_____

_____

_____

_____

_____

_____

_____

_____

_____

Put your initials below if you are willing to make a commitment before the Lord to devote yourself to becoming a more authentic believer. Only place your initials in the blank if you are willing to take responsibility for the stuff in your life and to be transparent with others.

_____

Day 4

....

Obey and Follow

As you look toward the future, what is it that paralyzes you? What hinders you from moving in the direction God has called you to?

There is little we can say about the future, simply because it is a series of events yet to take place. Oh sure, we can dream about the future. We can picture ourselves living in a quaint home with a white picket fence, two kids, and a dog named Max running around the yard as we sip lemonade on the front porch.

We can also make plans for the future. We can invest money into savings accounts, college funds, and life insurance policies. We can take classes, check out travel books about dream vacations, and set goals to achieve at work in the next year. But when it comes down to it, there is one thing we simply cannot do about the future—and that is predict it.

Life is full of unexpected moments. And for most of us, even those of us who follow Christ, there is a certain level of fear associated with the uncertainty about what lies ahead. And here's the dark side of that fear: it's one of the most debilitating factors we face as we strive to live out God's best for us.

The purpose of today's time of study is to encourage you to live boldly despite the unpredictability of life. If you cling to the Lord, you no longer need to live in fear of the days ahead. He created you and designed the precise number of days you will live and breathe on this earth. He already has your entire future mapped out for you. All you have to do is obey and follow.

Let's begin our study in prayer. As we start our time together, I want you to know I personally struggle with fear about the future, especially when it comes to my children. Whatever specific fears you struggle with, bring them to the Lord. He already knows everything about you, but he treasures the sound of your voice and longs to hear you speak your concerns out loud to him. So take a few moments and be honest about your concerns and fears for the days ahead. Ask God to reveal any areas of paralysis that are currently hindering you and to give you the confidence to take on the future at full speed ahead. Ask him to make you fearless!

First of all, I'd like to spend a little time Scripture hopping. I want you to see for yourself how little we as mere humans will ever understand about the omnipotent God.

Week 6   Day 4

1. **Read the following verses and fill in the blanks.**

Job 36:26 (NIV): God is beyond our _____ .

Proverbs 3:5: Do not depend on your _____ understanding.

Ecclesiastes 11:5: You cannot understand the _____ of God.

Isaiah 40:13: No one can fathom the _____ of the Lord.

Philippians 4:7: The peace of God exceeds anything we can _____ .

(NIV: The peace of God transcends all _____ .)

There's no way around it—life is unpredictable. But as uncertain as this life is, you can be sure of one thing: God is totally and completely in control. He has a plan charted out for your life. He will get you to the destination he has in mind for you, but in the process he may take you through some pretty rough terrain. When you find yourself in the midst of those rough patches, your first response may be to sit down and refuse to go any further. The road ahead looks too bumpy, too rocky. And besides, your feet already hurt. The problem with sitting down, however, is that if you do, you won't get any farther in your journey with Christ.

Have you been there before? Have you sat down to take a break under the shade tree and then found yourself unable to get moving again?

2. **If you have been on a spiritual hiatus in the past (or if you're on one now), journal about that experience. What bogged you down in the first place? How did you manage to get going again (or what do you think it would take to get moving now)?**

_____

_____

_____

_____

_____

_____

_____

_____

_____

3. **Read the story of the rich man in Matthew 19:16-30.**

In verse 22, what does the young man do?

_____

_____

_____

_____

4. **What paralyzes this man from completely following God?**

_____

_____

_____

_____

What or who do you feel is paralyzing you from bold obedience to Christ today?

_____

_____

_____

_____

_____

_____

_____

_____

This young man departed from Jesus very sad. He could have walked away rejoicing, had he only been willing to sacrifice for one Master. We, too, find ourselves grieved when we attempt to serve two masters.

We don't know if this young man ever turned away from his flesh and came back to Christ. If not, he may have died as one of the wealthiest men on earth—but in the end, he was still buried in the dirt.

There is an important lesson we can learn from his life: we must obey God unreservedly—completely, sacrificially.

5. **Read Matthew 9:9.**

Here is a man who hears the same call from Jesus but has a very different response. After Jesus speaks to Matthew in this verse, what does Matthew immediately do?

_____

_____

_____

Write your initials below if you are willing to fully obey and follow God no matter what the cost. By putting your initials in the space provided, you are saying to God, "I desire to live for you alone." Come before God right now, and tell him one thing (big or small) that you have sensed him calling you to do but you have allowed fear or worry to prevent you from going forward with. As you sign your initials below, commit to pursuing that dream starting _now_!

_____

Day 5

Audacious Faith

Contrary to what the world may tell you, the point of life isn't success or fame or popularity or financial security. As a child of God, you should make it your ultimate goal to lay your head on the pillow each night, knowing that you spent the day fearlessly proclaiming and living out God's Word to a watching world.

As we walk through our final day of this study together, please understand that your adventure with the Lord is only beginning.

Let's begin by praying in celebration today. I even give you permission to make a little noise before your Lord out of gratitude for what he has done within you over the past six weeks!

I fear that we as believers are just not excited enough about our faith and our Lord. Seriously, I have seen grown men who ought to know better paint their faces, rip their shirts, and scream like a bunch of monkeys about a football game and then the next day sit stiffly in church, stoic and unfeeling. I have seen women go nuts over a shoe sale or a girls' night out but come to church like defeated toddlers learning to use the potty for the first time.

The Lord isn't looking for lukewarm Christians; he wants followers who are radical—completely sold out for him.

[Moses said,] "You must commit yourselves wholeheartedly to these commands that I am giving you today."
DEUTERONOMY 6:6

1. **On the following scale, place a mark where you feel your level of commitment to the Lord lies (1 being the lowest commitment and 10 being the highest).**

1 ————————————————— 5 ————————————————— 10
recliner-chair Christian   halfhearted believer   radical for Christ

2. **Read 2 Corinthians 11:23-33.**

List everything Paul has been through as a radical for the Lord.

_____

_____

_____
_____
_____
_____
_____
_____
_____
_____
_____
_____

It is one thing to want to be bold for Christ and another thing altogether to actually live for him no matter what circumstances come our way. That's what separates stagnant, halfhearted Christians from Paul-like radicals. Becoming sold out for Christ doesn't just happen by accident or overnight. We must be intentional about activating our faith.

Let's take a look at another rebel for the Lord who is a master at activating audacious faith.

3. Read Luke 1:5-17.

Even before John's birth, it was prophesied that he would be filled with _____ .

4. Read Mark 1:1-8. John was a radical in every way—including what he wore and what he ate.

What did John wear in the wilderness?

_____
_____
_____
_____

What did John eat in the wilderness?

_____
_____
_____
_____

John's message was anything but lukewarm.

5. Read John 1:19-34.

John states that his life purpose, the reason he preached and baptized, is to make whom known?

_____
_____

John didn't just have head knowledge; he actually acted on what he believed. And in doing so, he prepared the way for Jesus' arrival.

6. List the specific areas of your life that make it difficult for you to activate bold faith for the Lord. Do they include a relationship, a group of friends, an attitude, an addiction?

_____

_____

_____

_____

_____

_____

_____

_____

_____

_____

If you are feeling overwhelmed right now, longing for the immeasurably more that God desires for your life but not sure how to make that a reality, please take heart. The smallest ounce of faith on your part can turn your world upside down and inside out. Listen to Jesus' words to his disciples:

I tell you the truth, if you had faith even as small as a mustard seed, you could say to this mountain, "Move from here to there," and it would move. Nothing would be impossible. MATTHEW 17:20

Taking the smallest step has the potential to lead to one of the biggest mountain-moving moments of your life!

It is only when we fully surrender to Christ that we find our true identity, our unique purpose, and our greatest thrill. As we experience the power of his redemption, we begin to live out an audacious faith. And we finally learn to embrace our position as people who are unequivocally named by God.

I, _____ , proclaim that on

this date, _____ , I have been named by God! Through the power of Christ, I have overcome my past, transformed my present, and embraced the future he has planned for me. I commit to living a life healed by the power of his blood and surrendered to the calling of his Spirit.

How to Become a Christ Follower

God so loved the world that he gave his one and only Son, that whoever believes in him shall not perish but have eternal life.

JOHN 3:16 (NIV)

God Almighty is the very essence of love. He possesses a love that the human mind will never comprehend—a love so rich and genuine that he gave his own Son to die in order to pay the penalty for the sins of the human race.

All of us—believers and unbelievers alike—are in need of a Savior. Although we may do good things, there is nothing we could ever do to deserve his salvation. "Everyone has sinned; we all fall short of God's glorious standard" (Romans 3:23).

If you long for intimacy with your Creator, you must make a commitment not only to turn away from every debilitating sin in your life but also to trust God to be the Lord over every circumstance—past, present, and future. If you've never done so before, give Jesus control of your life, and ask him to dwell inside you. "If you confess with your mouth that Jesus is Lord and believe in your heart that God raised him from the dead, you will be saved" (Romans 10:9).

It would be my greatest privilege to say to you, "Welcome home!" From now on, you are a new creation in Christ. "Anyone who belongs to Christ has become a new person. The old life is gone; a new life has begun!" (2 Corinthians 5:17).

It is vital to your future well-being and your relationship with Christ that you don't stop at this commitment. This is only the beginning—from now on it is important to keep growing and maturing in your faith. I encourage you to do this by reading the Word of God each day and by getting connected with a local body of believers each week.

I also encourage you to pray—earnestly pray. Ask God for wisdom, direction, clarity, love, and strength. Ask him for whatever you need—big and small.

Hold tightly to his robe . . . and get ready for the adventure of your life!

About the Author

Kasey Van Norman is a Bible teacher who is passionate about people and the proclaiming of the gospel. As the founder and president of Kasey Van Norman Ministries, based in College Station, Texas, Kasey desires to be a fresh voice that bridges the gap between the church and the lost.

Kasey's teaching style, whether she's speaking or writing, radiates a refreshing authenticity as she reaches out to a generation that is tired of hypocrisy and hungry for transparent leaders. Kasey's ability to relate to others, as well as to promote supernatural bondage breaking, grows from surviving a lifetime of difficult circumstances. And she didn't simply survive; she was transformed when she came face-to-face with the love and grace of God.

Kasey is married to Justin, her best friend, college sweetheart, and the man who continually models the love and grace of Jesus to her. The couple resides in College Station, Texas. They have two children: Emma Grace and Lake.

Coming Soon!

Kasey Van Norman Ministries'
Raw Faith Series

CP0530